RIDING LESSONS

Things I Learned While Horsing Around

MICHELLE EAMES

Disclaimer

I am a rider, not a horse trainer. Please don't consider anything in this book as training advice. Instead, it is a book of reflection on my journey of living, learning, and laughing with horses.

Front cover photo: Carol Klar

ISBN: 979-8-9873221-0-9

Printed in the United States of America

For more about Michelle Eames go to: MichelleEames.com

Dedication

This book is dedicated to my instructors and teachers, both in human and horse form. Thanks to my parents, and especially my mom, who finally let me get a horse when I was 12 and supported my horse habitat as a teenager. Thanks to my husband who, while not a rider, continues to embrace my horses as members of the family.

Contents

Riding Lessons

A Marriage, a Horse, and a Chainsaw

My love of horses was renewed with a trail ride on a rental horse. I was in my late twenties, hanging with coworkers in a new town, when one of the women said, "Let's go riding at this dude ranch." I was in. I knew how to ride. I was enamored with horses as a child, was thrilled to get a horse as a 12-year-old, and rode through my teens. I planned to get a horse again someday, likely when I retired and had more time.

Several of us went for that ride on that dude string, through the fields and blackberry thickets of Western Washington. I don't remember the name of the horse I rode that day. I do remember the squeak of the Western saddle, the rhythmic stride of the walk, the total relaxation of moving with a horse. My addiction to horses reawakened. I must have this fix more often. It could not wait for retirement.

I found a local barn that gave riding lessons with their school horses. It was a great barn, good people, good horses, with many teenage and preteen girls beginning their own horse journey. I got lots of riding time in. It was pure joy. When you are connected to a horse, you can do things you can't do on foot, borrowing the horse's speed and strength. Taking a horse over a jump is like flying, like a moment on Pegasus. Other parts of riding are like ballet with controlled precise movements. Riding an extended trot is my favorite— power and speed that could go forever. On the good days, for a moment, I am one with the horse.

Soon, I considered buying my own horse. I had a good job. I could board the horse at the barn, although I worried about the expense. I knew the price of the horse was only the beginning of what I would spend. Horses eat money as if it were hay.

I delayed buying a horse and went on a vacation instead with my husband and our friend Lisa. We had all been in the Peace Corps together and were going back to The Gambia in West Africa to visit friends and our host families. Our trip to The Gambia was great, however our trip to another nearby West African country got a little hairy when there was an attempted coup d'état while we were there. We spent several days hunkered in a small

1

hotel, listening to big weapons going off, watching armored cars roll by, and coming close to running out of food. It was one of those frightening life-changing events, when you realize that life is short and who knows when you will depart this earth. We chatted about this as we hunkered in our hotel room, ducking low by the cement walls as the military vehicles drove by with conspicuous machine guns.

Lisa said, "If we get out of this alive, I'm going to ask my boyfriend to marry me."

I said, "If we get out of this alive, I am going to buy a horse, because life is short and you've got to have fun."

Doug said, "I've been wanting to buy a chainsaw, if we get out of here, I'm getting a chainsaw."

Obviously, we did get out of there, and I put my horse-buying plan into action. The local barn owner knew of a nice horse, a three-year-old started by a 4-H kid. His name was Sonny, and the owner let me try him at the barn. He was lovely. He was an uncolored Appaloosa (with no spots). He was a liver chestnut, dark red-brown, with a long white blaze. He was calm, brave, sensitive, and well-built with big solid legs and hooves. I love big hooves on a horse. Once I adjusted to the increase in horse prices since my teenage years, I bought him. I never looked back.

We renamed him Kodo. Kodo is the Mandinka (a West African language) word for money. Ever since buying Kodo, I have spent money: saddles, boots, boarding fees, vet fees, shoeing and trimming. It never ends with a horse. We moved from Western Washington to Eastern Washington, and of course, we needed a house with acreage, then a truck, and then a horse-trailer. Add in the cost of hay, an additional horse as a buddy for Kodo, more vet bills, fencing, and different saddles for the new horse. Horse people spend money on a horse like foodies on gourmet meals.

I have an old friend who said, "Animals are put on the earth to teach you things." That's true for me and the horses I've had the joy of owning and riding. Sometimes the things they teach you are as simple as, *I'll never do that again. It hurts when I fall off.* Other times it's a deeper philosophical lesson about consistent treatment and respect. Often, for me, horses teach me to laugh, both at myself and at them. There's no doubt that we need more humor in this world.

So It Began

If I couldn't have a horse, I could play in my grandparents' barn, the horse boarders' saddles nicely stored on sawhorses.

"Don't sit on the saddles. It's bad for them."

But no one could see us. As small children my cousin and I would sneak out and ride the saddles, chasing imaginary cows, Indians, cowboys. The smell of leather, the squeak of saddles. We tasted the horses' grain, too. Hard oats, tinge of molasses. Once there was a mouse in the grain barrel. We shoved a stick deep in the grain so it could climb out. Climb out it did on the stick all the way to the top. Then it jumped! That jump mirrored by my cousin and I jumping back squealing. Who knew mice could jump that far, like a tiny kangaroo.

Sometimes the horse owners would come and give us rides on Charlie, the nice horse, tall as a mountain, calm as a butte. Now that horse could take you somewhere!

Horse Crazy

My horse life started with the begging era. For as long as I can remember I loved horses and begged for rides every time I saw one. Luckily for me, two of my aunts owned horses, and would give me rare pony rides (leading me) when they could, eventually letting me ride independently for minutes at a time.

After years of begging, my mom let me get a horse when I was 12. Lesson learned: constant begging can work. Heather was my first horse, an aged palomino mare. She was the perfect first horse, except for one small thing: saddling. When I tightened the girth, she would explode, rearing and pulling back, breaking even the strongest lead ropes. We were never able to train this bad habit out of her. But lack of a saddle doesn't slow a girl down. I developed great balance from years of bareback riding.

My second horse, Joaquin, was a short, flea-bitten gray, part Arabian (Arab) gelding. Flea-bitten gray. Don't you love that phrase? It means little tan speckles like flea bites on a grayish white background. Joaquin taught me to love a ground-eating forward trot. He could trot for miles. His canter, however, was a different story. He had one gear: run as fast as you can.

My third horse, Roman Regards, was an off-the-track Thoroughbred, in other words an ex-racehorse. If Roman got overexcited, and he was nearly always overexcited, he would canter sideways down the road, through ditches, or even during parades. As a teenager, it was a blast! Now I would think twice. Roman was tall, gray, and gangly. Together we would jump over every log or blackberry hedge we could find. Jumping is like flying.

Horses make people smile. Even non-horsey people, like my mother-in-law, loved to visit and watch horses. We would walk over to the neighbor's friendly herd of broodmares and foals, pet them and admire their shine. The horses, even the young ones, would walk right up with the "happy horse" look.

There are few expressive muscles over a horse's face bones. All of their expressions come out in their eyes and ears, and sometimes a nostril will flare, or lips move. Their smile shows in wide open eyes and perked-forward ears. They capture all manner of joy, anger, and frustration in that limited range of motion. Even non-horsemen can see the "happy horse" look with ears forward and big eyes curious. It takes time and experience to learn the other looks, including the ears-back-I'm-concerned-but-listening look, or the snaky-necked ears flat back and teeth bared get-out-of-my-way look. Actually, novice horse people can learn the get-out-of-my-way look quickly, especially if they are standing too close the first time they experience it.

The horse bug hit me hard, stuck, and my mom said it kept me off the streets. The bug infects many people. Whether you are a horse-crazy teenager, or a cautious grandmother, horses can grab your heart. There's a connection. We're meant to be with them, and they with us. To paraphrase, and revise, Winston Churchill: The outside of a horse is good for the inside of a woman.

Heather Under the Apple Tree

Heather's coat was golden, warm as the sun
dappled like the shade of our apple tree.
I lay belly-down along her spine,
head on her soft haunch,
eating an early season apple—
sharp bites of green.
Rest and eat, mowing lawn with teeth,
clover crunching, step, clover crunching, step.
Each step drops and lifts my body,
prone along the horse's back.
We ride my twelfth summer, her twentieth,
until the day the dark truck arrives.
She loads in relaxed with three strong legs.
I feed her one last apple.

Michelle riding Heather.

Falling

Every rider will fall off a horse. It's not if, but when. If you haven't fallen off, you aren't riding right. One of my worst falls was when I was a teenager. I had a little part-Arab gelding, Joaquin. He had three gaits—walk, trot, and full-out gallop. He did not have a collected canter, and we were working on it. You work on a gait by doing it a lot. The horse's muscles get stronger and eventually he can be slower and more balanced. I worked on turning the gallop to a slow canter, by galloping until he was tired, usually in big circles in a big field. One day we were working in the hay field, bareback, and Joaquin had had enough. He bolted, a full out run. I headed him toward a treed fence line, knowing he would stop at that barrier. He ran full tilt toward the line, turned at the last second, slipped in the mud, and fell down, landing with my left leg under him.

He got up off me and grazed. I got up, slowly, to see if my legs worked. They did, however my knee hurt bad. There were no cell phones at the time. I was a couple miles from my small-town home, and my only way to get back was horseback. I found a stump to get back on that little horse, and we headed home. My leg really hurt, maybe it was broken. I took the short cut through vacant lots, silently crying the whole way. It was only when I got home to Mom that I truly bawled. We put the horse away and headed off to the emergency room. My knee was only strained, yet it earned me a pair of crutches. I have loathed crutches ever since.

That little horse. When I think back on where we rode, I'm amazed I didn't have more serious falls and injuries. There were no helmets then, at least not really protective helmets, and my horse was scared of big trucks. Not cars, not pickups but the big diesel trucks. Unfortunately, the options for riding in my hometown were mostly road riding.

There was a very busy and well-traveled road to my out-of-town aunt's house. There was a big shoulder beside the road, and although cars went by fast, it was pretty safe for riding and most cars gave a wide berth when they could. But there was one old guy in town who delivered gravel in dump trucks. I no longer remember his name, but I remember his face. It was a mean face with wrinkles from age and being outside, a wide nose, big ears, and gray crew-cut hair. It seems like every time I rode along that route, he would be hauling on it. I would hear that loud diesel rumble as that big rattling dump truck approached, feel my horse tense, and as the truck came by Joaquin would hop and spin a fast 180-degree turn in place. Joaquin would calm right down afterwards, the threat gone. That old man in his dump truck would never move over an inch, despite that long straight stretch of road with plenty of room to see and move. I swear he purposely stayed as near to the shoulder as he could out of sheer nastiness. Even with all our road riding, Joaquin never got used to big semi-trucks. I never fell off on one of those spins.

For Sale or Trade

We were a one-horse family, and I thought both my horse, Kodo, and my husband, Doug, needed a buddy. I went shopping for a bomb-proof beginner's horse. I spent a couple of months horse hunting and found nothing worth looking at. I was getting frustrated and saw an ad for a local ranch that produces working horses. At that time, I preferred English style riding, although I had nothing against a good Western horse, and I figured a well-used ranch horse could be just what I needed. I went out and looked at two four-year-olds.

Yes, I know the rule about not buying young horses for beginners—but these horses had miles and miles on them.

The owners showed me one horse that was nervous and flighty and another horse that was very calm. The calm one ground-tied (stood quietly without tying) for saddling. He casually picked his way through rocky country; had a good stop; he walked, trotted, and cantered both directions; and wasn't scared of cars. What more could I ask for?

I brought the short muscular quarter horse home and introduced him to my husband. We picked out a nickname for him: Mansa, which means king in Mandinka. A wise old friend once told me to be careful what you name a horse, because they will live up to it. I should have listened. Things went well for a while, except that Mansa did become king of the pasture, and my favorite horse Kodo got beat up regularly. But my husband liked the new horse and they got along well.

One day we hopped on for a ride. Doug rode Mansa with a saddle and I rode Kodo with a bareback pad. On a blind corner not far from our house a car came fast around the corner, Kodo shied, turned a 180, which sent me sliding off his side, and ran for home, riderless, as if he were the lead horse in a steeplechase. Mansa, excited to join the race, spun like only a cow horse can (Doug held on!), and galloped frantically down the road as fast as his short legs would carry him. Doug was gallantly holding onto the saddle horn, yelling whoa, pulling back, swearing, until the saddle began slipping to one side. By then I was on my feet and running as fast as my long legs would carry me, yelling at Doug, "Stop him, turn him, jerk on the reins!" I had to rescue my husband! I got him into this mess! I ran, watching as the saddle listed further on Mansa's chubby, round back. I ran, watching Doug falling, flying, arms flailing, rolling as he hit the ground. Still, I ran, watching as he got up and rubbed the gravel out of his palms. He wasn't dead!

I ran up, panting, "Are you okay? I was yelling at you to stop him!"

"I was fine 'til the saddle slipped sideways. I bailed. He wouldn't stop." Doug looked fine. The concussion didn't show up until the next day. We went to catch our horses. Enough riding for that afternoon.

Other little problems started showing up with Mansa. Remember how nicely he ground-tied? Turns out that he didn't TIE very well. He broke my hitching post and pulled back on many occasions. But the major problem was when just as I was lifting my leg across his back, he launched into a series of bucks. Now I've ridden horses that buck once, and keep cantering, or that try to buck, but really aren't very good at it. But Mansa was built like a bulldog, all muscle, with very straight angles. His legs weren't shock absorbers, they were jackhammers. I stayed on, bouncing and catching air with each buck, until I realized he wasn't going to stop bucking, he was truly trying to get me off! I needed to grab the horn and pull his head up—just as I was thinking that he threw in a twist and I was off, landing hard on my arm.

I had a bucking horse. Once I knew that, I could prepare, predict, and avoid the bucking by saddling slowly and calmly, then doing a gradual warm-up ride. But I wouldn't let Doug ride him. I found a neighbor who had ridden some, and she confidently came to ride with me. I would ride Mansa first and then my neighbor would have a good ride on him. Except for the one day when I ran in the house before doing the warm-up, and as I came out the door, I saw Mansa buck my neighbor off. She ended up with a broken tail bone. I don't know why she hasn't been riding with me since . . .

Mansa was no longer fun. He was work. I put an ad in the paper: "For Sale or Trade for Good English Horse." When people called, I was honest and told them his habits. One woman came to look at him, and really liked him, but was hesitant to buy a horse she thought would need lots of riding. Then the cowboy called. He was looking for a dogging horse. I had to ask what that was. It's the rodeo event where the horse runs up beside the cow and the crazy cowboy jumps off the horse and pulls the cow to the ground. Turns out short horses are perfect for this, and Mansa was only fourteen-and-a-half hands high with his shoes on. The cowboy came out to try him.

I let the cowboy saddle Mansa. He THREW the saddle on and wrenched up the cinch fast and hard—Mansa erupted into a major bucking rage. Impressive bucking. Professional bucking. Eventually he settled down, and I knew I had lost a sale. However, I told the cowboy I needed to ride him anyway, since I didn't want him to learn that bucking avoids a ride. I lunged Mansa on a long line until he was calm, then got on and rode him very quietly, with very light aids.

I got off, and the cowboy said, "Well, I guess I'll ride him."

"I can't promise he won't buck."

"It's okay, I ride bareback," he said confidently.

I thought, hey, cool, a guy who rides bareback, he must be a really good rider! I thought again. No, he means bareback broncs. Well, heck yeah! Jump right on! I figured he might be able to ride out those bucks. He could do the classic cowboy kind of thing.

He jumped on, and instead of giving a slight squeeze to move forward, he clicked his tongue and slammed his legs into Mansa's side. Mansa jumped forward, bucked hard, and the cowboy hit the ground. Mansa knew who was king.

"He was going toward that tree, I had to jump off," said the cowboy as he slowly got up. "I guess some horses just like girls better."

No sale, obviously.

By that time, I knew bucking was becoming a habit for Mansa and I knew it was too much for my limited training skills, not to mention my common sense. I was trying to figure out how to find a good trainer; maybe they could train him and sell him on commission. That same afternoon I got one more phone call from a 14-year-old girl who had a mare for sale for the same price as Mansa, and she wanted a good barrel and rodeo horse. Her mare had the wrong build for barrels. I told her not to waste her time and explained that Mansa had bucked a cowboy off that afternoon.

The girl laughed and said, "Yeah, well, he was just a cowboy."

The girl and her mom came out the next day. It was amazing—Mansa and the girl bonded. She made that horse do stuff I didn't know he could do. He didn't buck. She was calm and gentle with him. She loved Mansa!

Immediately I drove out to look at her horse, thinking that if it was standing on four legs and mooed, I would trade. The mare was a perfectly decent, slightly spoiled Arab/Appaloosa that could walk, trot, and canter both directions and wasn't scared of cars. We traded, straight across, for a thirty-day trial. I fell in love with the mare. She was calm, Doug could ride her, and her gaits were perfect for dressage. I was scared to call at the end of the trial period, in case they wanted to bring Mansa back. But they still loved Mansa and it was a perfect trade. The mare lived with us until the day she died and was the queen of our hobby farm. But we were careful not to name her Queen.

Her registered name was Wayjan's Shaykina, and her nickname when we got her was Shakey. That name just would not do, it sounded like a horse with shaky training that was unpredictable. The closest Mandinka word to Shakey I could find was the word for shiver: kissi kissi. This was a much better name, and it fit because she was also a mouthy mare, always looking for treats in your hands and pockets. These were rather like kisses, so Kissi was appropriate. Kissi lived up to her name: she gave us kisses that turned into nibbles that could turn into bites if you didn't watch her. We could handle that kind of habit.

Michelle on Kissi, her Aunt Cathy on Kodo.

Kodo's Secret Life

Our hobby farm has two acres, a nice two-stall barn, and good fences. Well, adequate fences. We started with my Appaloosa gelding, Kodo, and eventually settled on an Appaloosa mare to keep Kodo company—I mean for my husband to ride. My horses have a good life with a roof over their heads in the winter, grazing in the summer, and room to run. I even manage to ride them now and then. In the summer I rotate the horses around the subdivided pastures and am always dumping, filling, and moving multiple water buckets.

One day I found a bird in a half-empty bucket. I'm a professional wildlife biologist, so was able to examine the bird closely, and determine that yes indeed, it was dead. I could see no evidence of foul play, and assumed the poor critter dropped in for a drink and couldn't get out. Death by accidental drowning. Later events, however, caused me to question that conclusion.

In addition to horses, we raised poultry of various kinds. Our first batch of birds was twelve banty chicks that we bought through the mail and raised on our back porch until the dust from their scratching got so thick that we thought we had been translocated to coastal Washington for the fog season. It was time for my yearly house cleaning, so we moved the chickens out to a pen in the middle of one of the horse pastures, where most of the chicks grew and thrived to become a colorful troop of banty chickens. The cutest ones were the palomino-colored buff cochins, with feathers down to their toes, like little trousers. These were also the most mellow and tame chickens: little Buddhist chickens, who often stopped to meditate.

Sometimes, especially in windy weather—about every other day around here—my horses would run around like maniacs when I tried to catch them. I know it is hard to believe that Appaloosas would have independent and contrary opinions, but it's true.

One day the horses were in the pasture that held the chicken pen, and the chickens were ranging loose, nibbling on flies in the horse manure. I had the urge to ride. I grabbed a halter, walked into the pasture, and Kodo perked up his ears, winked at the mare, and began one of his crazed rampages, bucking, rearing, running and snorting in circles around me as I stood in the center of the pasture, waiting for him to quit showing off. The mare, of course, had to join in to get her kicks, and to keep out of Kodo's way. Chickens were running, flapping, and squawking everywhere, which added to the joyous chaos of the occasion. I was just shaking my head, examining my fingernails, waiting for the show to end, when out of the corner of my eye I saw Kodo, head down, nose pointed at one of the buff cochins, aiming right for it: splat. One 1300-pound weighted hoof met chicken. Chicken pancake. Pasture kill. I couldn't believe it. Surely it was an accident!

I could picture the headline: *Giant Running Horse Randomly Stomps Slow Meditating Chicken.* Eventually the horses mellowed, I buried a chicken, and went for a ride.

The third suspicious incident occurred a couple years later. We decided to raise three turkeys—one for Thanksgiving, one for Christmas, and one as an extra, just in case. Domestic turkeys are notoriously stupid and have been known to die of such things as looking up at raindrops until their nostrils fill with water and they drown. The deal was that my husband and I would raise them, and my brothers-in-law would butcher them. I don't do butchering.

The turkeys grew and grew and grew over the summer. As they grew, their super-sized breasts and drumsticks became more and more ungainly. They waddled, working hard to carry their weight, like a television wrestler on steroids. But we still liked to let them out to graze and eat the slower bugs so they had some joy in their lives. One day the turkeys were grazing, and I brought Kodo into the pasture to free lunge.

Free lunging with an accomplished trainer is a very controlled exercise where the horse, with no tack, circles around you and reacts to subtle changes in your body language, thereby learning to focus on you. Free lunging when I, a non-accomplished amateur backyard horsewoman, do it, is more of an exercise in wild abandon, somewhat controlled by my yelling, arm-waving, and swearing. I usually gain significant insights during the process, mostly things like, *Wow, Kodo, you sure are pretty when you buck!* or *Glad I'm not riding you right now!*

Kodo was cheerfully cantering in a circle around me, enjoying the exercise, when the turkeys began moving into the field, innocently grazing and heading toward their pen, oblivious to the half-ton liver chestnut tank barreling toward them. *Uh-oh*, I thought, as Kodo came around the bend, and the big tom turkey lumbered into the path, eye on a blade of grass. Kodo pretended to try to avoid the turkey, and actually jumped over him, but his hooves clipped the turkey and rolled him over. It was like a semi-truck on Interstate 90 side-swiping a garbage can.

I resignedly caught Kodo, tied him up, and came to gather up the 35-pound crippled turkey. He couldn't walk. He just lay there with missing patches of feathers. He flapped wings in my face as I picked him up. I heaved him into the pen, near food and water, wondering if he would make it through the night. I checked on him early the next morning. He was alive, but still wasn't walking. He needed butchering, my husband was out of town, my brothers-in-law lived three hours away, and I had never butchered a bird in my life. I called my retired rancher neighbors to assist. Three hours of blood, guts, feathers, and yellow jackets later, the turkey was in the freezer.

I now believe Kodo was a serial bird killer. I tried to rehabilitate him with long trail rides in the woods. Sometimes a pheasant or grouse would flush right in front of us, and Kodo would jump or shy sideways. I am unsure now if it was true surprise, or delight and anticipation of the thrill of the hunt.

My husband and I moved on to raising ducks, which wandered the property more than our other birds. We had four ducks, then lost one. I blamed coyotes at the time. However, in retrospect, I wonder. Did Kodo kill the drake? Was that shallow depression in his pasture actually a shallow grave? Was that mud or blood on his hooves? Was Kodo only pretending to be a rehabilitated criminal, ready to revert at the next opportunity? After all, he was an Appaloosa.

Coffee Pot Bend

I have been blessed with horses that are hard to fit with a saddle. Cursed may be more appropriate. It's like that Greek guy that has to keep pushing the boulder up the hill, he almost gets to the top, and it rolls back down again. The boulder is the saddle. I have bought and sold many.

Kissi was one of my saddle fitting challenge horses. She was built like a barrel with legs. When the saddle pinched, she wouldn't take her correct left lead canter. With assistance from my very meticulous dressage teacher, Patricia, I tried saddles, returned them, and shopped some more until I found one that appeared to fit. I was giddy with delight at finally finding a good saddle. The delight would be short-lived, each time I eventually found it still pinched Kissi's shoulders. Back to the bottom of the hill for more saddle shopping. We tried a Kieffer dressage saddle that seemed close, though in the end it wasn't right. Each saddle in the search process was more expensive than the last. We tried a Passier Nicole dressage saddle. The Passier finally seemed like a good fit for Kissi, it was stupendously comfortable for me, and luckily, it also fit my other horse Kodo.

It was time for one of my intermittent summertime trail rides with the neighbor ladies who knew every trail within 20 miles, knew every landowner, and had permission to ride on all the nearby private land. They thought a six-hour trail ride was short. I tacked Kodo up with the new dressage saddle, figuring that perhaps my butt would be less pained at the end of the ride than usual. That day was a long jaunt to Coffee Pot Bend. Coffee Pot Bend turned out to be a bend in a large creek where supposedly some old-timers in the neighborhood used to ride and stop to make coffee.

Two hours into the ride, right at Coffee Pot Bend, we had to ford the creek. Kodo was a great horse, with a good mind, but he hadn't yet experienced everything in life. Tina and Ruby crossed the creek on their horses, and Kodo and I followed. The water was over his knees. He hesitated, I cued him in, and he stood in the middle, pawed and splashed enough to get my boots wet, and then walked out. I briefly worried about my new saddle; however, it hadn't gotten wet. I proceeded to rave about how wonderful Kodo was, and how it was the deepest water he had ever crossed. Tina and Ruby smiled, and we continued on.

A quarter mile further down the trail we had to ford the creek again. This time Tina's horse Buster balked. She, not wanting to lose an argument, insisted he go in, and stand in the middle. He eventually did so, and the water was close to his elbow. Kodo was a big horse, but Buster was bigger. Ruby and I were beginning to discuss whether we wanted to cross or not, however by that point Buster and Tina were on the other side, and Ruby's horse Paka decided that where Buster goes, he would go too. In Paka went, without hesitation, and crossed. Paka was a little horse and the water went over the top of Ruby's cowboy boots. That left Kodo, me, and my new dressage saddle on the wrong side of a stream. This was only my third ride in the saddle. But I figured, at most, only Kodo's belly and girth would get wet, and maybe my boots. Besides, if little Paka could do it, we could too!

I urged Kodo forward and grabbed some mane for security. He stepped in with his front legs. He pawed the water. Took another step. Looked at his buddies on the other bank. Stepped . . . and thought, *OH MY GAWD THE WATER IS DEEP. WHAT'S GOING ON?* Instead of stepping through and out, or even jumping, it was like he thought he had to swim in this elbow-deep water. Suddenly his legs collapsed, he got ready to swim by crouching and the crouching/ducking movement caused a large tidal wave to come crashing over his withers, over my thighs and over my practically new Passier Nicole saddle. Then Kodo, strong athlete that he was, bounded out of the creek in one jump, and was on top of the steep bank in another jump, to be welcomed by Tina and Ruby, both laughing. We took a break to empty our boots of water. Kodo, the saddle, and the saddle pad were soaked. There was no choice but to ride the wet saddle several hours home. Everything dried okay although where my wet breeches were rubbing against the saddle, the leather roughened and stained. Fortunately, after the saddle dried, many applications of saddle oil made that area nearly invisible.

I never told Patricia, my strict dressage instructor, about the saddle and creek event. She would not have approved of getting the saddle wet. Teachers don't have to know everything. I did confess to my more laid-back jumping instructor. She said it was not uncommon for green horses to think they have to swim in somewhat deep water. The moral of the story is saddles dry out. Oil hides stains. Dressage horses need to get out in the world.

As I think back on this ride, I understand why the locals called this spot Coffee Pot Bend. Their horses probably did the exact same thing; however, they were prepared with matches, a coffee pot, and coffee, and took the time to dry out their boots a bit before heading down the trail.

A String of Bad Luck

People with horses get to know their veterinarians. It comes with the territory. But one fall, I got to know my vets a little too well. I never thought that my barn and pastures were unsafe—although in a perfect world I would replace some of my wire mesh fences. That fall it wasn't the old fences that got the horses in trouble, it was human error and horse error. (Okay, really mostly human error coupled with typical horse behavior.)

One Sunday in October during what I knew would be the last good weather of the fall, I was out trail riding on Kodo and thought I would take a shortcut home up a really steep hill. Unfortunately, at the top was some old rusty sagging barbed wire. I considered going back down the hill to take the 3-mile loop trail home, however Kodo was a calm horse with a good brain, and I knew if I stood on the wire to make it lay flat on the ground, he would cross it.

Unfortunately, it didn't work as smoothly as I thought, and he got caught, panicked a bit, and tore up his hind legs around the stifle, canon bones, and above one pastern. The injuries bled, but he could walk.

By then we were still on the wrong side of the fence, and we had to cross it again. No way was I going to make him take the longer way home with abrasions and lacerations all over his legs. The second time he successfully crossed over and I saw that he likely wouldn't bleed to death, and I could lead him the mile and a half home. The cut above the pastern was deep and open, so I called the vet on a Sunday afternoon. I figured the big emergency vet bill would lessen my guilt, anyhow. The vet agreed one laceration needed stitches. He cleaned and sutured the wound. "Keep him in the stall for a week," he said. Kodo hated the stall.

I had to travel for work, and my husband took care of him the next Monday night and Tuesday morning. On Tuesday, after Doug went to work, Kodo found a way to unlatch his stall, escape, and pull open the door to the barn, where he ate about 15 pounds of grain, some alfalfa hay, and went for a walk around the neighborhood. The neighbor called Doug, he came home from work, caught the wayward horse, and went back to work.

I got home from my travels that evening and Doug told me what had happened. I sized up the remaining grain, reviewed the horse first aid book, and immediately started walking Kodo while worrying about colic (a mild to severe intestinal blockage). Sure enough, in an hour, Kodo had major colic symptoms. He had a distended stomach, and he was trying to roll due to the pain.

The vet finally arrived and put a tube through his nostril and down into Kodo's stomach, causing sour smelling, icky greenish water to flow backwards up the tube. That was a bad sign. Kodo's stomach and sides were very distended from the fermenting grain. The vet poured mineral oil down the stomach tube to settle things and lubricate the system. Kodo was given drugs for pain and inflammation, and I walked him off and on, and by midnight he was passing manure, a good sign. I continued walking him every hour through the night.

By the next morning Kodo refused to walk. I called the vet; he thought laminitis might be starting. Laminitis occurs when toxins from colic cause the capillaries deep in the hoof to basically explode. It is extremely painful for the horse and can have additional long-term complications that affect the bony structures in the hoof.

The first day the vets treated the laminitis with pain killers. It was worse by the second day, with pain so extreme I was getting mentally prepared to put Kodo down. Once the vets were sure the digestive system was working again, they really threw the drugs at him to treat the laminitis symptoms. They took X-rays to see if the coffin bone inside the hoof had rotated due to internal structure damage. It hadn't, thankfully, since that could mean permanent lameness. As a preventative, they taped rubber wedge pads on his front hooves to elevate the heels. In addition, my husband and I hauled and shoveled loose sand into the stall for Kodo to stand in to keep the toes pointed down and put less stress on the coffin bone. Kodo made very slow improvement and in a week he was standing with less pain. So far, so good. During yet another visit the vet squeezed Kodo's front feet with hoof testers (giant pincher-plier things) and he did not show pain, showing that the coffin bone was still in its correct position. Hooray!

By the end of October, Kodo was starting to act like my favorite horse again, including trying to find ways out of his stall. We increased the security by adding new stall latches, making sure the hay storage latch was always locked, and moving the grain completely out of the barn and onto our enclosed porch. Kodo had no obvious lameness, and we gave him some time off to heal.

About the time Kodo was feeling better and was turned back into the paddock with Kissi, we started seeing unusual destruction to the barn. At the time our two stalls had open doors into the paddock, with both horses having free access to either stall or the paddock. Dutch doors from either stall faced into our yard. One day in late October Doug came home from work and found the two horses grazing in the yard. They had walked right through the lower Dutch door of Kissi's stall. The door was split down the mid-line and pushed out with the hinges holding one side, and the latch holding the other side. No injuries. We nailed a piece of plywood over the opening and waited until the weekend to rebuild the door.

A few nights later, I was getting ready for bed and heard a big crash. I ran outside to see what was up. The horses were in the yard again, happily grazing. Kodo's stall door was flat on the ground, like in a cartoon where someone opens the front door, and it falls flat into the living room. I eventually caught both horses; they were giddy with delight at being out. Luckily, they had no injuries, and I locked them out of the stalls and went back to bed. The next day Doug rebuilt the doors, using much longer screws on the hinges. By Saturday night we had reinforced doors, reinforced hinges, and reinforced latches. We kept the top half of the Dutch doors shut until I had time to string electric fencing along the fronts and middle of the stalls. I assumed that Kodo was the door breaking horse because he's muscular and solid. He must have figured out how big he was and just pushed. Later events made me wonder if it was Kissi.

Originally, our stalls were one big, open area. To divide it into two stalls, we put a tubular metal gate in the middle. Voila! Two stalls. The first week in November Kissi went into a very obvious heat. When a mare goes into heat, it often makes her moody, kicky, and/or stupid. We started having incidents with the divider gate. One morning the chain holding the gate closed was broken, the gate was open and pushed to one wall, and Kissi had a gaping, one-inch laceration above her right front pastern. Of course, this required another vet call.

By this time, I knew both my vets well. We were on a first name basis, and often joked, "Long time no see!" The vet explored the wound and it was surprisingly deep—more of a puncture. Kissi got stitches, and some pain killers, and we were told to keep the wound dry. The stitches looked good when the vet made his return visit. Things were looking up again!

However, we had two more incidents where the horses knocked the stall divider/gate off the hinges, although without injury. Another morning we found that part of the barn wall had been kicked off the foundation at the door corner. Suddenly I understood why the really nice horse barns are made out of solid oak rather than 2x4s and plywood. It's not just for beauty. That next weekend our barn repair duties included building a real wood wall between the two stalls, running electric wire above the new wall and above the two Dutch doors, with the hope of keeping the horses away from the edges. The stalls were a spiderweb of electric wire. I blamed the problems on Kissi being in heat and thought they'd just go away when the hormones decreased. (You may be thinking by now that I'm naive and a slow learner.)

Despite the web of electric fencing, we had another stall incident where Kissi jumped partway over the bottom of the Dutch door and got high centered, belly over door, causing a multitude of abrasions, with a resultant vet visit at 2 a.m. on a Sunday morning. Now that was an expensive vet bill.

Finally, I figured it out. The horses had to be separated at night. This was actually a surprise to me, because they will calmly eat off the same hay pile and play with each other like best friends when they're in the field or paddock. If there was space to move away, all was well. The problems only showed up when they were crowded in small areas. Horse herds are hierarchical. There is always a boss, and a pecking order. Usually the boss is a mare, however in my herd of two, the boss was the gelding. If Kissi was in a stall next to Kodo's stall, all was fine. But if he tried to come into the stall that she was already occupying, there was no easy escape, and she would go over or through any barriers.

Horses are powerful when they are panicked. A more experienced horseperson would have seen the problem long before I did. As a temporary fix, Kodo was banished to a different pasture. The next weekend, in yet another round of barn reconstruction activities, we reconfigured the fences so that there were two separate paddocks with access to only one stall each. Hooray for easy electric fencing!

That should have been it for unpredicted vet visits. There should have been no more injuries. Problem solved. But on the first Friday in December, we came home from work and Kodo's right eye was swollen half shut. I was sure it would heal overnight, so I left it alone. When I got up early Saturday morning it was no better. I woke Doug so he could be the horse-holder (he loves that!). With a lot of difficulty, I got a good look at the eye. I saw a little divot on the surface of the cornea. This was an injury, not an infection. I read my horse first-aid aid books again, which warned me to be really careful with eye problems and not to ignore them. I called the vet. Again. He eventually made it out on Saturday afternoon. The examination showed it was a corneal ulcer, commonly known as a divot on the eye. Further exploration showed no foreign bodies, so the vet prescribed eye drops four times a day.

The vet warned me that horses have extremely strong eyelid muscles. By gosh, he was right! Kodo, good boy that he was, didn't pull his head up out of reach, or freak out and pull back, he just closed his eye. It took Doug and I some serious effort to get it open just a bit to drip some drops in there. After two days Kodo was significantly better, and after an additional day we stopped the eye drops. I learned from this injury that the direction of the eyelashes is an indicator of pain—eyelashes pointing down indicate problems. We thought that the cause of the eye injury may have been windblown dust or grit. At least this vet visit couldn't be blamed on human error or horse behavior. It just happened.

In total that fall our vets came out once for barbed wire, nine times for the colic/laminitis incident, once for Kissi's laceration, once for teeth and vaccinations, once for Kissi's stall door high-centering incident, and once for Kodo's eye injury. That was 14 vet visits between early October and early December. I am still kicking myself for not figuring out the basic horse behavior/crowding issue sooner. Ever since then I have made sure that if my horses need to be contained, they have a separate safe space. But out in the pasture, they can still play, chase each other, and run with abandon. I'm sure they won't have any accidents.

Fence Building

My fences have an unpracticed look about them. I understand the mechanics of fence building, the laying of the guide string, the pounding of the posts, then pulling, stretching and tacking up the wire. My electric fences divide my pastures, yet they wander. Like horses grazing, there is a randomness to their direction. My fence poles are placed far apart to find soil between rocks. I search for giving spots, the soft between the hard. I meander, to make the shortest distance between two points a long hike from tree to low spot to high spot, working around basalt clumps. I build a leaning, weaving drunk of a fence, a serpentine around intentions, a straight line drawn by a snake. Still, my fence functions, holding in the horses most days, until the deer jump and pull down an electric strand which shorts out with a pulsing *tick-tick*.

Kissi's Dressage Show

Dressage was my favorite riding discipline for years. Dressage is like dancing with the horse, where you use subtle aids to ask the horse to do flowing and perfect movements at all gaits. There are several levels and you progress your way up through the levels. Your skill in each level is measured through individual dressage tests. The arena is marked with a letter system to define where figures in each test begin or end. The movements are ridden at different gaits and include circles, turns, diagonals, or straight lines. Each piece of the test receives a separate score, all of which are added up for the total, much like figure skating.

The lower levels include Introductory, Training, and First Level. Those are the levels I had experience with. There are several higher levels that move up to the very advanced Prix St. George. Introductory is quite simple, comprised only of walk and trot. Prix St. George has impressive movements like trotting in place and canter pirouettes. I loved riding dressage but was ambivalent about showing.

Kissi was my best horse for dressage, and my instructor, Patricia, had been suggesting that I show for a year or so. I never seemed to be quite organized enough to commit. Kissi and I had been having major disagreements about the necessity of cantering on the correct left lead while circling to the left. Details, schmetails! One summer it clicked, and we figured out the left lead canter. We probably were up to the correct canter depart a good 65 percent of the time and were getting better by the day. I finally signed us up for a dressage schooling show and discussed the appropriate tests with Patricia. She suggested the easy Introductory 2 test just to get the horse in the arena, and Training Level 1 and Training Level 2. For several lessons we practiced parts of the tests, and she lectured me on my position and frowned at our transitions, the moment of changing from one gait to another. They don't call it Training Level for nothing—we did *a lot* of training.

For weeks I tried to memorize those ridiculous tests. Is this the one where I do trot circles at either end of the arena with diagonal crossings between? Canter transition right before or right after C at the end of the arena? When was I supposed to do the canter-to-trot transition? Somewhere before the beginning salute in the center and the end of the test, I presumed. I practiced in my head. I practiced on paper. I read the tests before I fell asleep. I read the tests during my lunch break at work. I rode the tests on my other horse, so Kissi would not begin to predict the movements. Finally, at my last lesson before the show, I was beginning to get it. If I concentrated on one test for 5 minutes, I could ride it all the way through. I rode Training 2 for Patricia at the end of my lesson, and she complimented our ride, a rare thing. She proceeded to lecture me about grooming and trimming my horse and presenting a neat and professional appearance. No matter what happened, I was supposed to make the show a pleasant occasion for the horse. I liked this advice. It took all the pressure off.

We arrived at the show on Saturday as directed, about an hour and a half early. My mom and husband were there to act as grooms and support staff. As I led Kissi around she was high-headed and looking everywhere. Did I mention she's half Arabian, and like most Arabs loves looking at things? Nonetheless, she was very obedient. We groomed her, put clean white polo wraps on her lower legs, and I warmed her up in a muddy arena. There went the white wraps. Our first class was running half an hour late, so we had lots of time to look around, and ride the nervousness out of her. The last ten minutes before the class I stood at the indoor arena gate and memorized my Introductory 2 test, again. I glanced in at the previous rider, saw that she was riding a different test, looked away to avoid getting confused, and then it was my turn.

We entered the arena and walked around the edge to the scariest part, the judge's end. The judge's table was extra scary to Kissi because this was a Halloween show and the judge wore a witch costume. Kissi looked at the flowers displayed around the arena. Kissi looked at the video camera. The bell rang, to indicate the time to begin, and we started the test at the far end, trotting, and halted in the center. I tipped my head in a salute. We trotted forward, turning left at the judge's end of the arena, making a circle at the side. As I passed the judge again, she called out, "Michelle?" I thought this was strange since one doesn't talk in a dressage test. I answered, "Yes?"

While I continued circling, she said, "You're riding the wrong test."

Whereupon I responded, "No way!" and she explained that the introductory tests had just changed. It was an easier test, in fact. By now I was walking to the judge's table and we continued our impromptu conference. She explained this new simple test to me, an explanation that lost me at the second figure. I asked if perhaps I could get a reader and she called a very organized pony club girl in to read the test out loud for me. We started over. We rode the test adequately and ended up getting a fourth-place ribbon in a class of five. I thought, wow, things can't get any weirder. Luckily, during our mid-test conference, the judge explained that my other tests had not changed, thus my memorization was not a total waste.

After a break, I prepared for my next class. This time for the warm-up I put spurs on, since Kissi had been excessively sluggish in the first class. I warmed her up, reminded her that "leg" means "go forward." We got two out of three correct canter transitions to the left during our warmup. Pretty promising! This time at the arena gate I was reassured that the competitors were riding the same test that I had memorized. Phew! At last, it was our turn.

We trotted around the arena until the bell rang, and we entered at working trot, and halted in the center to salute the judge. The judge, now wearing her witch's hat, bowed her head back to me. Kissi focused on the strange black cone moving on the judge's head. We started forward at trot, and Kissi began to slow down to stop and take another really hard look at that scary black cone. I could feel she would not trot to the end near the judge, so while we were still capable of forward movement, I cut the corner early to make it to the next figure. Kissi had now changed from lazy to hyper alert, and I was frazzled by her shying. The good part is we had some really lovely energetic movements. The bad part was that I almost forgot the test, and at one point started to circle in the wrong location, and then corrected myself. Our canter circles started out well, then changed to a discombobulated cross-lead canter. These were not perfect circles and it was not our best ride. Still, we ranked third out of four horses and got another ribbon. The judge was generous.

By the last test I was tired. But this was the test that I had found easiest to memorize. I took advantage of the lunch break to ride and explore all the nooks and crannies in the arena. One more test and then I would get to go home. Hooray!

We entered the arena, and at the salute the judge only tipped her witch's hat slightly. We rode the test with no shies, no wrong leads, and no significant errors. Kissi was trotting well, she was listening, and she was energetic. We finished the test, and both Kissi and I were smiling. I was thinking, *That's my girl!* and she was thinking, *Isn't it time for a horse cookie?*

We got second place.

So, we did it! One wrong test, one rotten test, and one good test. We would be Prix St George in no time. Of course, this was just before winter, and we would likely forget everything by spring. We never did excel in dressage. But Kissi sure had a lovely trot. It was like a power boat, at the perfect speed when the bow just lifts out of the water, and the movement feels effortless. All those dressage lessons were worth it, just to feel that power trot.

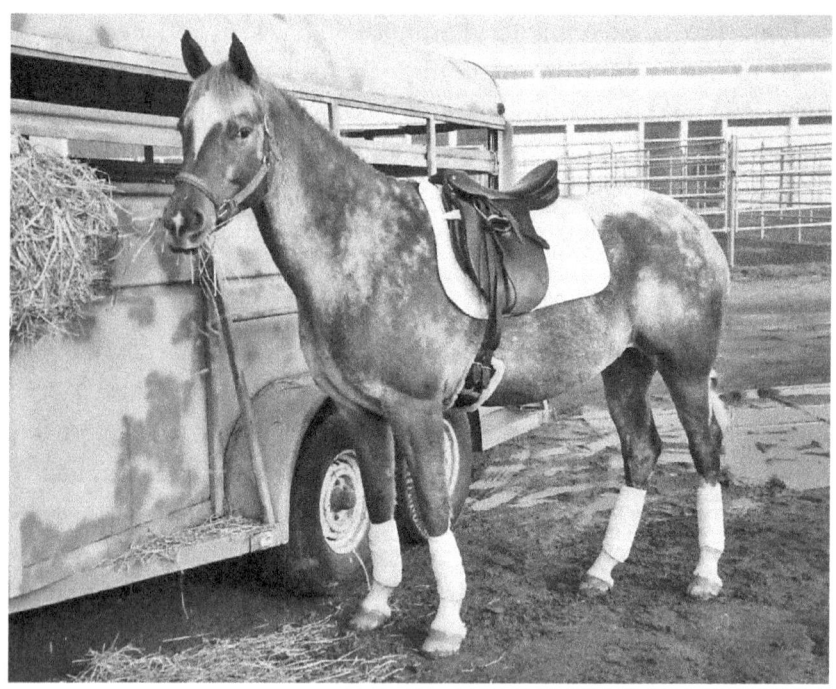

Kissi at the dressage show.

Braiding

I braid hope into my horse's mane
one inch at a time
braid band sew,
knot into a button
braid band sew.
I thin the mane with a blade
instead of pulling hair
from live twitching flesh
(like I was taught, out by the roots)
blond bird nests at my feet.
Barn swallows make nests
of hair and mud in eaves
horses paw nests in straw,
once our mattresses
were stuffed with horsehair.

Reading My Horse, One Saddle at a Time

She tells me which saddles pinch in subtle language—stiff canters, breaking gaits, wrong leads. Each saddle of our journey costs more; we climb a mountain of discarded saddles, littered with hundred-dollar bills of regret. Now, I'm ordering a custom saddle made for me, made for the horse, made for bankruptcy. Almost silly for this amateur rider, but Kissi needs a ride with no pain. I need to sell a saddle at a loss again.

Horse Breeding, Vegas Style

When I was five months pregnant and using rubber bands to connect my riding breeches' snaps over my bulging belly, I decided to breed Kissi. The plan was a guaranteed moneymaker, or at the very least would provide me with my next dressage horse. Plus, it would give Kissi something to do while I was pregnant and dealing with a young baby.

I researched stallions that would complement my mare's good points and counteract her bad points. Kissi had upright, well-proportioned conformation for dressage, and a beautiful, naturally elevated trot. The stallion should, too. Kissi was short, had slightly turned in hocks and was opinionated like all good Appaloosas. The stallion should be tall, with straight legs, and have a calm, hard-working temperament.

I drooled over gorgeous stallion pictures in magazines, considered German horses with frozen semen shipped across the ocean. I oohed and aahed over stallion videos, asked advice about heat cycles and breeding, and grew a big belly over the winter while Kissi grew a big belly from good hay and minimal riding.

At last I decided on a Hanoverian stallion, Wyatt Earp, that lived just an hour away. The stallion only did artificial insemination, and given my inexperience with horse breeding, having experts do the job at the breeding farm was the way to go. I sent in the $850 stud fee and a deposit for the breeding barn. The stud-fee came with a "live-foal guarantee." I couldn't wait to see my own live foal.

Kissi always showed very obvious heat symptoms, such as squealing, kicking, and flirting with geldings. That is, until the year I decided to breed her. In early spring I waddled out to the barn daily only to see Kissi's normal and typical reaction to my gelding's approach: pinning her ears, snaking her neck, and threatening bites. Finally, in late February she turned her rear toward my gelding and raised her tail. As advised, I waited twenty-one days for the next cycle. Then I waited thirty-one days. Then fifty-one days. And then two months! Nothing. I had my baby, Mac, in April. In late May I hauled Kissi and my month-old baby to the vet. Both appeared healthy and the ultrasound showed Kissi was near ovulation: do not hesitate, do not pass go, haul her immediately to the breeding farm. My excitement overcame my new-mom-exhaustion as I paid the vet his $250 and headed out the door. My money-making scheme had begun.

We left Kissi at the farm, and she finally ovulated a week later, with help from a hormone shot. I picked her up, read my "Mare Owner" instructions, and waited fourteen days to bring her to the vet—hopefully to confirm pregnancy. Another ultrasound: not pregnant. But she looked near ovulation! I paid my vet his usual $250, and this time I waited until the next day to haul her to the farm. I hauled her home a week later. At fourteen days the vet did another ultrasound—not pregnant again. With Mac snuggled in his front-pack I explained to Kissi that I had not had any trouble becoming pregnant. What was her problem?

In late June we tried a third time. "June is the most fertile month!" the stallion's owner explained enthusiastically. I left Kissi at the farm, hauled her home in a week, and by the next week goo was oozing from her vulva. Add in a four-day treatment for an infection ($520). The vet bills and farm bills were turning my money-making plan into a bankruptcy. By July, it was time to go back to work to support my horse habit, buy some hay, and ride Kissi for a change. We would try again next year.

By year two of our breeding adventure, we had celebrated Mac's first birthday, and I was riding more regularly. So much for "giving Kissi something to do" while I was saddled with a new baby. Unfortunately, Wyatt Earp was across the state in training that year, and they would be shipping frozen semen—an expensive change of plans at $500 a pop for shipping. Kissi had an early heat in February and then finally another heat in May. At least, I think she was in heat, her only outward sign was being nice to my gelding. I brought her to the vet, he checked her cycle ($170), then we timed the semen shipment with her likely date of ovulation. The semen, when it arrived, showed very low motility, a complicating factor. If she were easy to breed, it wouldn't be a problem. But she was not easy to breed, she did not get pregnant, and we tried again– second try, second year, second shipped semen, second "not pregnant."

It was time for damage control. The stud fee, farm fees, vet bills, and shipping bills were breaking my budget. I could resell the stud fee/breeding and cut my losses, I could find a mare to lease with a good breeding history, or

I could buy a brood mare. Like I needed another horse! I put feelers out to sell the breeding opportunity. I looked around at a couple of potential mares for lease. One mare was cute and pregnant (a miraculous condition, I thought) and could be leased the next year. I found a whole herd of Thoroughbred mares to pick from, although they were maiden, and aged. I wanted a proven broodmare. I talked to the owner of another Thoroughbred broodmare. She didn't want to sell her mare, but she really needed the money. As she put it, she was horse rich and money poor. Mac and I drove out to look at the mare called Pocket Change. She was big, black, had a good walk and an okay trot. Then she galloped. Her rear legs reached up all the way to her belly, and in one stride she was in a full run— perfect propulsion for dressage. I liked her. Pocket Change had produced three babies. We made a deal: I would buy the mare for $1,000 dollars, breed her, and likely sell her back to the original owner when I had a foal on the ground and the owner had money again. I went home happy and laughing at myself. I bought more hay ($400), and now had three horses to feed for the winter and pet on the nose. Things were improving.

By the third spring of our breeding adventure Mac was two. Pocket Change showed very obvious heats. We hauled her to the breeding ranch in May ($380), brought her home the next week, and crossed our fingers.

Did I mention that I work part-time? Part-time that spring became a crisis-oriented full-time-plus, and I forgot about the fourteen-day-after-breeding visit to the vet. I wasn't worried, it was still early in the season, and Pocket Change hadn't come back into heat. I finally got her to the vet in late June for an ultrasound and palpation. YES! She was pregnant! But wait, another fetus. Twins. Horses rarely carry twins full term, and if they do, there are often difficulties. If I had brought her in at fourteen days, the vet could have pinched one before it implanted in the uterus. After implantation, pinching one will usually harm the other. So we terminated the pregnancy ($420). I felt like I had put my last quarter in the slot machine, two cherries popped up, and the third jackpot cherry slowly slipped by. At home I had a talk with Pocket Change and told her she was an overachiever—easy to get pregnant—however she'd gone a little too far.

I learned some more reproductive biology that third year of trying. If you wait too long before terminating the pregnancy, the mare won't cycle back into heat. We tried to stimulate her with estrogen shots. No luck. So, I quit for the year, bought hay, rode a little, and petted my three horses on their noses.

By the next spring two winged horses were kicking it out in my head. The romantic Pegasus coaxed, "This is it, one more breeding and your Olympic-caliber foal will be frolicking across the pasture!"

While the practical Pegasus prodded, "Enjoy the horses you have! Get out! Save the money from more vet bills, ultrasounds, hoof care, and foal care. Go to Vegas, buy a boat, or feed your green directly to the horses! Anything but horse breeding."

The practical Pegasus whinnied louder. I called Pocket Change's previous owner and sold her back at the original price, with a good deal on the stud fee. I breathed relief when Pocket Change left the property and took my horse breeding dreams with her. It was a small price to pay to learn important lessons. Okay, it was a big price to pay, however I still learned some lessons:

1) You don't make money on horse breeding,
2) Breeding horses is a game of chance, and
3) There's always next year.

I just need a little luck, a lot of money, and another pull of the lever.

A friend just called and told me about a real nice deal: a broodmare with a foal on the ground, and she's bred back to a stupendous stallion. The owner wants to sell, cheap.

Gotta go! But don't worry, I'm just going to look, not buy.

Horse Shortcuts for Working Moms

Once upon a time, I was a double-income-no-kids kind of woman, learning dressage and jumping. I had two great all-around horses, a healthy middle-class paycheck, a supportive husband, and all the daylight hours I could spare to ride after work. At one point I was hauling horses to two lessons a week, riding between lessons, and loving every second. With planning, I could afford a new (used) saddle, good breeches, expensive bits, shavings in the stalls, tune-ups on the truck, and other horsey necessities.

Then I got pregnant. I actually rode through the seventh month, due to mellow horses and an easy pregnancy. Mac was born, and after six weeks, I asked my doctor when I could ride again. He laughed and said just get some sleep. I rode after nine weeks. That first summer was catching rides when I wasn't catching naps, or catching up at work, or catching up on the house, and catching my son smiling and chattering and touching all things new. I became the queen of short cuts and quick rides. My horse time was sacred. I needed this time for sanity breaks and to be alone and breathe. I kept my horses at home, so it was easier to run out for 15 minutes and run back in. I had mellow horses, so there were things I could do that might be unsafe with more unpredictable animals, like leading a horse while carrying a baby in a backpack. Mac's first word was "Dad." His second word was "Whoa."

Some of the shortcuts I figured out during that short-of-time period of my life follow. Even if you board your horse, some could still apply.

Skip the shovel, sometimes.

If your horse is locked into a stall, you need to clean stalls every day. But if your horse has free access—cleaning can slide a few days. Just avoid feeding hay on top of manure. I mean, think about it, would you eat off a dirty toilet seat?

Do the brush off.

Brushing the horse where the tack sits is critical and shouldn't be ignored. But tail brushing? Brushing a tail breaks the hair, so don't do it too often. I read that somewhere. That's advice I can live with.

Grin and bare it.

Ride your horse. That's why you bought him. But if you're comfortable, ride bareback. Or learn to ride bareback. Saddling takes up precious minutes of riding time. Personally, I only ride bareback in an enclosed area, but every ride counts!

Short timer.

Short rides are better than no rides. Become the queen of fifteen-minute rides: a quick body brush, helmet, bridle, ride, go in and start supper. Fifteen minutes can get a horse warmed up and you can practice a few focused things. See Grin and bare it.

Dark as the night.

Ride after dark, when hubby is home, and kids are in bed. Only in safe enclosed areas. Stay on your property, and off the roads, unless the area's well lit, and the roads aren't busy. My horses have a great time riding out in the pastures. We mostly walk. Not recommended for goofball, young, or psychotic horses.

Exercise the guilt.

Walk or lunge your horse. When I feel short on time and am getting no exercise myself, I take a horse for a hand-walk with a halter and lead rope. Leading your horse in a halter "counts" for horse time, you get exercise, and your kids can come too. Sometimes the whole family "walks" the horse.

Toes up, heels down.

If you want to learn toes up, heels down, ride in clogs or other backless shoes. Ride without stirrups. Your toes will be up to keep those shoes on.

Monitor communications.

Ride in a pasture right by the house with a baby monitor while baby naps. This only works with the right set up, and if you are able to trust the horse, pull off his bridle, and run at the first cry while he grazes.

Make it a family affair.

Ride while husband bikes with bike trailer and baby. This was one of my son's favorite activities. Plus, my husband got exercise, too.

Dump the kids and grab the horse.

Ride while your husband is home. You deserve an evening off. Get out of the house and spend quality time with your favorite horse. Swap babysitting with another rider. This would work best if horses were at the same barn. Pay a barn teenager to watch kids while you ride. Invite Grandma to visit and go for a ride. Grandma didn't come to see you, anyway.

Take the kids to the barn.

Bribe kids with yummy snacks and favorite toys. This depends on your child's personality—my son would sit on the bleachers and watch me ride a lesson. Park the kids in a clean stall or the back of the truck with toys while you groom and tack up. Don't expect your instructor to watch your kid but warn the instructor to wear her boots as she may be riding. If my son deteriorated into crying or wandering, I let my instructor ride. She learned about my bad habits, and the techniques that work best on my horse, resulting in better instruction.

Take the winter off.

I don't mind riding in cold or wet weather. But if there's a lot of dangerous ice, it's a no-guilt reason to hang out with the kids and give the horse a break.

Share your horse.

Do a half-lease with another rider. Set up clear schedules, and ground rules, and work as a team to keep that horse fit.

Respect your elders.

This is a good time to focus on your mellow, aged horse. He'll think he's on vacation or gone to horse heaven. Just food, light rides, and walks down the road with the human family. This is not a good time to start a two-year old under saddle, nor is it a good time to put mega miles on.

Be a kangaroo.

Lunge horse with baby or toddler in a backpack. Mac loved this, and he loved the long blue whip that can double as a pretend fishing pole. Avoid child whip-play near the horses. Just sayin'.

Bring a friend.

Bring a friend to lessons. Ask them to hold the baby. I did this; some friends loved it, some felt taken advantage of. Guess which of them are still my friends? All of them, though some didn't babysit much.

Hire it out.

Hire help if you can afford it, but not necessarily for riding. Hire someone to clean your kitchen and bathrooms, so if you have a free moment, you can go pet your horse on the nose. More fun than mopping the floor!

Don't feel guilty for taking time off from the kids. Your kids are the hardest job you'll ever love and your time away will give you energy when you return. You will model caring and respect for animals, and your kids will learn from you. If you're lucky, your kids will become horsemen. Also, if you're lucky, they won't become horsemen and your horse time will continue to be your personal escape time. Either way, you are showing that true art, and true horsemanship, takes patience, a long-term commitment, and love. Don't be surprised if they pick soccer or dance or music instead. The same passion applies to other activities, and you'll have taught them well.

Escape

Three women ride up the hill
horse hooves quiet on the damp gravel,
laughs in the sun.
Women escape their houses,
horses escape their pastures:
a walk in the pines.

Pig Problems

My friend Sandy and I often visited back and forth. We lived hundreds of miles apart yet enjoyed traveling to opposite sides of the state to experience different weather. One spring I visited Sandy and her daughter, and they took me to meet a friend with a Haflinger pony. Haflingers are draft ponies and are very solid and heavy. I was intrigued by the breed and really wanted to meet one. I was loving on the mellow pony, not paying attention, when she stepped on my toe. It hurt bad. I pushed her off and suffered through the rest of the visit with a probably broken big toe. But I ignored it, because doctors rarely treat broken toes and I knew it would heal in time.

The same summer our neighbors got pigs. They kept the two pigs way back in the corner of the property, adjacent to our fence line. I learned my horses were scared to death of the pigs. Doug was injured once when Kissi freaked out coming through the gate near the pigs. She jumped and knocked him into the fence. We fixed that by avoiding the issue. We moved the back gate to the other side of our property. I spent time working my horses in the pig corner, trying to get them used to the pigs. The horses never relaxed. I've been told that because pigs are omnivores they smell like bears, like a predator. Few horses like them, and I didn't know the right training techniques at the time to get the horses over their fear.

Not long after our visit to Sandy's house, she, her teenage daughter Christina, and their dog came to visit us. I was bringing the horses out to pasture: Kodo on a lead rope and Kissi following loose behind. We were in a narrow electric fence alley as we headed for the pasture near the pigs. Sandy's dog rushed out of the tall grass, surprising the horses. Since the horses were already on heightened pig alert, they shied from the dog. Kissi jumped forward to get past Kodo, knocked me over, stepped on the arch of my foot as she jumped over me, and the collision threw me out of my clogs. Horses were running, frantic, and I was stunned and really hurt, wondering if I had a concussion. I lay on the ground and wondered if I could make it to the house. I wondered how long it would take Doug, Sandy, or Christina to notice I was missing. I wondered if the horses would come back to check on me. I finally sat up, slowly and carefully. I stood, crouching, weight on my good foot. I tested my bad foot. It was excruciating but I could walk cautiously. I limped into the back door of the house, and yelled out for Doug, crying. He came downstairs and helped me to a chair. Christina came in, looked at me, her eyes got big, and she ran to wake up her mom to help.

Doug and Sandy insisted I go to the doctor, where they x-rayed me, and checked my pupils for a concussion. There was no obvious concussion. The technician who reviewed my x-ray saw a break in my big toe. I explained that was an old injury, from the Haflinger. The new injury was on the arch and top of my foot. The technician made a note on my chart and said a radiologist would read the x-ray and get back to me, but it didn't initially look like any bones in my arch were broken. Nonetheless, they put my foot in a temporary cast, and gave me crutches.

I was on crutches for several days. Luckily Christina was there to help because my son Christopher was a baby. Carrying a baby with crutches was impossible. It got very old, very fast. Finally, the doctor's office called back with the official x-ray results.

The first call, from a nurse, went like this:

Nurse: "We wanted to let you know your toe was broken."

Me: "Yes, I know. It was broken a couple months ago. What about the arch? Any bones broken in the arch?"

Nurse: "All I have is a note from the radiologist saying your toe is broken. I can't say anything about the arch. And we don't treat broken toes."

Me: "I understand you don't treat broken toes. That's why I didn't come in for treatment months ago for the broken toe. Do I need to keep this cast on for the arch that may or may not be broken? Crutches and a baby are pretty challenging."

Nurse: "I'll have your doctor call you."

The next day I get another call: "Hello, this is Ruth for Dr. Smith's office."

Ruth, I know Ruth. She's the nurse for my kids' pediatrician. She's older and has seen everything.

Me: "Hi, Ruth, I recognize your voice. You are my kid's nurse."

Ruth: "Yes, I'm filling in. They make us work all over. I was asked to call and explain that your toe is broken. We usually don't treat broken toes, but we can fit you for a hard shoe if you want."

Me: "Ruth, that's an old injury. My horse ran me over and stepped on my arch on the same foot. Do I need to keep wearing this cast? Babies and crutches don't mix."

Ruth: "They have you in a cast?" (Big belly laugh!)

Me: "Yes, and I want to get it off. What can we do?"

Ruth: (More loud laughter). "I'll make an appointment with a Physician's Assistant. She'll take a look."

I went to the appointment, they removed the cast, and we tried various braces, ending up with a laced ankle brace to keep my foot straight and support the arch. We laughed through the appointment about how everyone got waylaid at the obvious broken toe, assuming that was the problem, and never finished reading the chart.

It was similar with my horses. I thought the problem was obvious—the pigs. But if you dig deeper, look closer, and really read the horses, it turns out the problem is really obedience and submission. We didn't need to move the gates. We needed to move the horse's feet away, so they never ever crowd us or run us over. It took me a couple more years to really learn to do that with a horse.

Pets and People

We've all heard that dogs often look like their owners, but what about horses? I used to think my favorite horse Kodo didn't look like me but looked and acted a lot like my husband.

If Kodo were a human he would veg out on the couch, drink beer, and watch football. Beer comes from grain, after all, and taking it in the liquid form is easier than chewing. Kodo was built like my husband: solid, stocky, with big feet and a friendly face. They both had the same mellow, agreeable, and generous heart. They both loved to eat and were easy keepers. It didn't take a lot of fancy food to keep them in flesh.

My husband and Kodo worked hard when they needed to work and rested hard after. Kodo may have had more mechanical aptitude than Doug: he could untie his lead rope knots, and quickly open most stall door latches. For all their brawn, both Doug and Kodo could dance through their athletic activities—Doug on the baseball field or golf course, and Kodo in smooth and sensitive sideways leg yields and other movements.

Both animals, husband and horse, tended toward stubbornness. Kodo would stop at major trail junctions, especially where there was a choice between a long way home and a short way home. He gave me several opportunities to choose the short way. Doug would consider my advice and do what he wanted anyhow.

My mare Kissi was not like my husband, or me, or my dog. She was a mare unto herself. She was pretty, in a voluptuous, movie star kind of way. She had an adorable broad Arab face, and she would toss her strawberry blond mane as if to say, "I'm cute, let me do what I want." If horses look and act like their people, she must have been owned by Marilyn Monroe in a previous life. Or perhaps by Miss Piggy.

A Horseman's Thermometer

For everything there is a season. For every season there is a temperature.

10 degrees and below.

The hose freezes when trying to fill the trough, even if you carefully drained it the last time you used it.

18 degrees.

Nose hairs freeze. Wet hair freezes stiff on your head when you feed horses after a shower. This temperature is only good for running out for the morning paper and feeding the horses. It's still cold even while wearing a sweater, down coat, hat, long johns, jeans, Sorels, and big mittens.

30 degrees.

I can ride in this. With long johns, jeans, sweater, and a coat it's almost bearable in the sun. Stay inside if it's raining or blowing.

40 degrees.

Still cold, but rideable. Skip the long johns, keep the coat, hat, and gloves. Lighter gloves are okay.

50 degrees.

Practically gardening and barbecuing weather! Unzip the coat. This is great fall riding weather.

60 degrees.

T-shirt and jeans if you're moving, long sleeve shirt if you're standing still. This is the best trail riding weather in spring.

70 degrees.

T-shirt and shorts, to show off your pale white horseman's legs while doing barn chores. Tank top and jeans while on a horse. Remember to carry water on the ride, for you, and water in the trailer for the horse.

80 degrees.

Horse people are outside all day. Horses sweat immediately. Carry two bottles of water on your ride.

90 degrees.

Ride in the morning, then retreat back inside. Spray down the dust in the horse paddocks.

100 degrees and above.

It's too hot to ride. Air out the house at night and close it off in the day. Drink iced tea and eat popsicles. Get out the kiddy pool for the dog. Fill the horse trough. Spray off the horses with the hose when they walk up asking for a shower. Find the air conditioner, watch movies, and wait for a change in the temperature.

Fall Riding

Lately our summers have been full of smoke from wildfires, cramping our riding style. But fall in Spokane can have amazing weather. Often, we get cool yet sunny days, colorful trees, and the winter weather holds off. It reminds us of why we live here, and why we trail ride.

One friend was saying she almost wished for bad weather in the fall so she could rest and catch up on inside chores. Really, no one can complain about fall rides. The inside chores can wait.

Even during the nice autumn weather, the nights get colder and aren't so great for camping. My friends and I were discussing the end of camping season, and that we would have to wait until spring to expose our young horses to more camping experiences. Did we really have to wait? Who says we can't keep training our horses to be good camping and trail horses for the next season?

Things we can work on at home to prepare for camping season:

1) Tying.

> A good camping horse must tie well, whether at the trailer, on a high line, or on a hitching post. Horses learn to tie, by, well, tying them. Tie them in a safe place, and gradually increase the time you leave them there. At my house I have a hefty fence post, the trailer, and lots of pine trees to set up a high line. Even if the weather isn't great for riding, I will tie a horse while I do outside chores. Don't tie them to a trailer that isn't hooked up to a truck, because horses are strong enough to pull it. Also, don't tie an inexperienced horse to a tree where they can twist around it and panic. If you have a horse that tends to panic while tied, contact a trainer.

2) Respecting an electric corral.

> The first time I took my horse camping, I didn't know if he would stay in an electric fence corral. Luckily, he did. Wouldn't it have been great if I practiced at home first, to be sure my horse was

ready? You can do that in the fall and winter. Set up your small electric corral, or small panels, and practice. Leave the horse for increasing amounts of time, or even all night. For the first overnight experience, you may wish to do this inside a larger perimeter fence.

3) Simulating trail experiences.

When you can ride on those nicer days, practice the things you'll need on the trail. Take a jacket on and off (start from the ground if you have an inexperienced horse). Purposely bump against tree branches to make that scary, scratchy, tree-brushing noise. Drag things. Put the pack bags or saddle bags on and clean up the garbage along your neighborhood roads and fields. Hang flags on your fence and stalls to blow in the wind.

4) Shop early for Christmas.

You might accidentally find some cool camping gear for next season. Buy it, because life is short and you need presents, too!

5) Practice your camp cooking.

This especially works if you are in a place where you can have an outdoor fire. Enjoy the cool evenings, clear nights, stars, and Dutch oven cooking. Camping season is just around the corner!

Trucks

Now that the spring flood has somewhat diminished, and I can get the horse trailer out of the mud, my mind turns to trucks. A horsewoman without a truck is like . . . stuck at home. If you don't have a truck and trailer, and you want to trail ride, you need to make friends with someone who does. Oh, and teach your horse to load. You'll be glad you did.

I started hauling my own horse when I was 16, because my mom and aunt got tired of hauling me to lessons and 4-H events. I would haul my horse with my aunt's trailer, and her boyfriend's old truck. It was an old Ford, a 150, I think. It had compound low gears and really loose steering. The steering wheel would wobble six inches to the left and right, without moving the truck wheels. It was tricky to keep it in the driving lane on narrow roads. The gas gauge didn't work, and I had to calculate the gas in the tank based on the odometer, the gallons put in, and the estimated miles per gallon, coupled with distance needed to haul. One time I miscalculated. Whoops. I had to be rescued. In that era before cell phones, that involved hopping a freeway fence, and knocking on a stranger's door to borrow a phone. I lived to tell the tale.

After my teenage years I took a break from horses. When I got a horse again, I needed a truck, especially when it came time to move across the state. My friend sold me an old stock trailer, and I found a 1976 Chevy truck, a "camper special," with a 454 engine. That engine made the coolest deep bloop-bloop sound. It had the old push-down radio keys with retro ceramic knobs. Unfortunately, the radio didn't work despite its cool vintage look. Back when I was in high school the kids used to tease those of us with small imported 4-cylinder cars and talk about the treadmill under the hood with a squirrel running to power the tiny engine. This blue Chevy truck didn't have a squirrel, it had a big pig on a heavy-duty pig treadmill. The pig ran steady, with stamina and power, and he was really thirsty. He sucked on a straw connected to the gas tank, and the gas tank was filled with beer. He drank about a gallon every eight miles, unless it was uphill. Then it was a gallon every six miles. That pig didn't care whether the truck was hauling or empty. It just traveled steady, and sucked beer. I mean gas.

The old blue Chevy pulled the trailer well for several years, but you had to know its idiosyncrasies. For example, the battery cables often needed cleaning or jiggling before it would start. Even then it was hard on batteries, and it needed a new battery every spring. If you needed to drive it on a cold day, you had to plug in the block heater. I think that was to get the pig warm so he could turn the treadmill. Alternatively, if you had to drive it on a really hot day, you had to use the old-style air conditioner, otherwise known as a wing window, pulled all the way in to vent the sauna-like wind at your face. I loved that truck.

Eventually, the old blue Chevy got more unpredictable, so we upgraded to a newer (though not very new) rig, a white Ford 250 with a full crew cab and an 8-foot bed. I swear that truck was 40-feet long. I regularly ran over curbs and snowbanks when taking corners. I did better with the horse trailer attached, because I was used to swinging wide, however if you turned me loose with just the truck in downtown Spokane . . . look out street signs! Pedestrians waiting for the walk signs better watch their feet.

That truck did have some cool electrical stuff, some of which actually worked. Like the cassette player. Mind you, we were well into the era of compact discs by then. The electric key fob thingy only worked on the driver's side door, and we had to do that old fashioned thing of reaching way across the seat to unlock the passenger doors by manually lifting the lock. But that truck could carry six people with lots of elbow room, and it had pulling power and tight suspension for hauling a load. It was really only happy and smooth with a camper and a loaded horse trailer. Plus, it had a working air conditioner! Except for that one time in the middle of the summer, on the way up Mount Spokane. And the other time after that. Around then we determined we needed a new truck.

Our current truck is a red Chevy 2500 with an extended cab, not a crew cab. It has some Gucci electrical stuff, and most of it works! We have also changed out the trailer from a 3-horse slant to a 2-horse slant. I swear we decreased our truck and trailer length by 15 feet! Okay, maybe it was only six feet, but think of how much more maneuverable this hauling rig will be up at the trail heads. This truck seems more dependable and predictable than the others, and I'm ready to hit the trails . . . although I have to tell you, I really miss the sound of the motor on the old blue '76 Chevy.

Trailer Things Fall Apart

I learned many things about horse trailers in my formative years of hauling. From my Aunt Theresa, I learned that trailer wiring can be really funky, and mess up frequently. I learned that the state patrol and sheriffs will pull you over for that kind of thing, and the tickets cost money. My aunt had so much trouble with the lights working erratically on her trailer, that she had it completely rewired with some thick, heavy-duty wire. I also remember watching my dad spend hours working on his boat trailer wiring, testing and retesting connections. At least with horse trailers we don't back them down into corrosive salt water. Hopefully. I prefer my aunt's approach to wiring, though; pay a professional to redo the whole system.

Based on my family history of trailer wires going bad, I check my lights every spring. This is a two-person job, one controlling the lights, and one watching all the lights from outside: running lights, turn indicators, brakes, and back-up lights. I test them before my first haul in the spring. If something isn't working, it might be a bad bulb, or it might just need jiggling, and if it's worse than that, I find a professional. After that first check in the spring, I don't check too often. If I get pulled over by a cop, I want to be able to say in good conscience, "The lights were working last time I checked!" I do have friends that check every haul, every time. That's probably a safer idea.

My aunt's trailer was a 2-horse straight load, with two pull-down ramps that acted as the back doors. I hated those ramps. If they were put down on uneven ground and the horses backed down them, the hinges would torque and make them very difficult to close. We were always putting rocks under the ramp ends to level them and brushing manure and dirt out of the giant hinges so they would close tightly. These days I prefer the more common step-down trailers; there's one less thing to break.

One year I splurged and bought a brand-new trailer. Not a fancy trailer, but a very functional trailer. I bought it late one summer and had the plug-in-thingy changed out to fit our old truck. Shortly thereafter, we bought a new-to-us, not-as-old truck. When we plugged the trailer in, the brakes would lock up on the trailer. We were basically dragging the trailer down the road with locked wheels. It was more of a sled than a trailer. I am not particularly mechanical, but I was pretty sure that wasn't good for my trailer tires. Of course, this was the day before a long-planned horse camping trip. I found a nearby mechanic, and we drove the trailer unplugged with my mom following in her car on the smallest back roads we could find to sneak the rig into the mechanic's shop without being seen by a cop. The mechanic was great. He fixed it by the end of the day. It turns out it was a malfunctioning "sending unit," a little computer gizmo on the truck side of the wiring system. Who knew such things existed?

Then there are trailer bearings. These are inside the wheel, inside those little rounded hub thingies. I used to have a horse that would paw when tied and regularly knock the hub thingies off the wheels. They popped right back on my old trailer. I was once told that the bearings should be checked yearly. Again, I use a professional, since I only vaguely understand what the bearings are for. Having bearings checked, greased, or changed is not a cheap thing, however, it's worth it to avoid catastrophic breakages.

When my elderly horses were pasture pets and I had been hauling infrequently, I had a trailer that was showing its age. The walls were rusting out down by the frame, and it was ugly. I thought it needed some sprucing up. I figured we could sand blast it and paint it. Surely, I could pay someone to do it. I called one guy I found on Craigslist, who said sure, he could do it for a thousand bucks. I thought it was odd that he didn't ask me any questions about the trailer's condition. I called another established trailer repair company. The representative asked for some pictures. When I sent those along, he said it didn't look good, and I should haul the trailer down for a safety inspection. The end result was that the rust spots were basically beyond repair, my floorboards were rotted out, and I should not put a horse in it. Repairs would cost more than it was worth, so we took everything useful out of it and scrapped it.

With my new trailer, I pull out the mats every spring, sweep and brush the grit and dust off, and paint the floor boards with wood preservative. I wish I could paint the preservative on the underneath side, too, but I haven't figured out how to do that yet. While the mats are off, I inspect the wood, and poke it with a knife to see if it's still solid.

I think that trailer tires are more likely to go flat than any tires on any vehicle I've ever had. My old stock trailer tires all seemed to have slow leaks.

I was always pumping them up. Did you know if you haul on one low tire, at 70 MPH, for an hour, that the rubber wears off the tire? I didn't use to. Now I do. I'm lucky nothing worse happened. And you must check your tire pressure. I learned that you can buy air pressure indicators. Pushing the indicator onto the tire valve stems causes it to display a color code for the pressure range. I'm sure they aren't super accurate, though they do tell you if the tires are really low. I have also learned that the new tires on my new trailer hold air so much better than on my old rig. Until the day I ran over a nail.

Long ago, when I moved from Olympia to Spokane, I bought an old horse trailer from a friend in Olympia, and an old Chevy truck. As I loaded my horse up at my friend's farm, I said I was nervous about hauling alone across the state. My very experienced friend said, "Don't worry, if something happens, horse people will stop to help you." I made it across the state, without a breakdown, unless you count the truck alternator malfunctioning. You can drive quite a ways on a bad alternator. If you don't need lights. Or turn indicators. Anyhow, I always remember what she said: horse people help horse people.

One day years later I was driving home from work and saw an old horse trailer with a horse pulled over on Highway 2. I remembered the rule, "A horse person will help." I was a horse person, so I pulled over. The back wheel was crooked on the trailer; something was definitely wrong. A young yearling horse was inside. The mom and daughter had just bought the yearling at a horse sale and she was barely halter broke. I told her we were only four miles from my house and if she could limp the trailer that far, we could get the filly to a safe place and then she could deal with the trailer. After some discussion of other options, she followed me home very slowly. The mom parked the rig, unhooked, and headed home to North Idaho. In a couple days her husband completed replacing the broken axle on the old trailer, loaded up the filly, and took her home. I felt good that I was able to follow through on one of the commandments of horsemanship, helping another horse person in trouble. I also vowed to regularly maintain my trailer to avoid future broken axles.

Fully Loaded

My husband assists me with horse loading by holding the back trailer door open as I lead my horse up and walk in, the horse easily following. The worst my horse does now is pause at the back of the trailer, as if asking whether I'm serious. For the worst pauses, I swing a rope toward him, or get a whip to tap his haunch, and he steps in. But this is nothing. My husband has never dealt with a true hard-to-load horse. He has never dealt with a horse falling in a trailer, either. My husband has no idea how strange, frustrating, or worrisome loading and hauling can be and how lucky we are to have good horses.

When I was a teenager, my aunt and I would haul to riding lessons together. My mom would come along for company. At the time, I had Heather, a lovely beginner's horse. Unfortunately, she was very unbalanced in a trailer and would wobble around at every corner. You can feel a horse moving in a trailer, it transmits through the hitch and up to the truck. You can feel it a lot when they are really swaying or thrashing around. One day on the way home from a lesson with Heather and my Aunt Theresa's horse Killer in the two horse, side-by-side trailer, we felt a large crash as we went around a corner. We pulled over to the shoulder to check. We peeked over the back of the trailer. Heather had fallen down. Her big body filled up all of her side of the trailer floor, her chest scrunched against the front, and one rear leg stretched dangerously underneath Killer.

Theresa and my mom pondered what to do. I worried. Heather looked hopelessly stuck. We opened up the back ramp. Heather wasn't struggling but she couldn't get up in that tight space. We knew we had to get Killer out first. The black mare's nickname was Killer because she would kick for any little reason. We had to back this grouchy mare out of the two-horse trailer over my horse's leg, and hope that she didn't step on my horse, adding a broken leg to our problems.

Just as my aunt was considering turning the rig around to haul over to the nearby, old-timer cowboy's place, a local dairy farmer drove up and stopped to help. He looked at the situation, scratched his head and said, "You know, if she was a cow, she'd be up by now. Horses lurch forward to get up. Cows get up back-end first." Calmly assessing the situation, the old farmer agreed the black mare had to come out.

Theresa carefully unhooked the butt chain behind Killer and asked her to back up by tugging on her tail while standing safely to the side. Killer hesitated, and slightly shifted her feet. Theresa moved forward to the small manger door and got more insistent by pushing against Killer's head and loudly saying "Back!" Finally, Killer backed out very slowly, completely avoiding Heather's leg. My job was to hold Killer, letting her graze beside the road, while Mom, Theresa, and the farmer considered their next steps. Having a job kept me from imagining the worst.

Heather's butt and tail were at the back edge, just perched over the ramp of the trailer. Heather was laying calmly through all of this. She was a good horse, she just had poor balance. The ramps were partially in the road, and there was a ditch next to the road. The divider between the side-by-side trailer stalls was welded in place with no way to move it. There was a 2-foot opening at the floor level, with a solid panel above.

"I think we just need to pull her out of here. I'll hitch a rope to her front, you ladies can pull on the tail, and we'll get her out," said the farmer.

I was watching and listening and trying not to cry.

He looked over at me and said, "Horses' tails are very strong. Don't worry."

Like all good farmers he had a long rope in his truck. He tied the rope to Heather's halter, and up around the divider for leverage to pull her upward. On his command, the farmer, my mom, and my aunt pulled rope and tail with all of their strength. Heather's weight shifted, and she finally got her butt out on the ramp, sliding out and rolling over sideways into the ditch. She stood up in a panic, jumped out of the ditch toward a barbed wire fence, and stopped. Theresa caught her and she seemed mostly unhurt with just a few scratches. She was walking on all four feet. We thanked the farmer, and then had to load the horses up again to get them home. Surprisingly, they loaded easily. We drove home very slowly around the corners.

At least Heather and Killer were easy to load. So many horses that we hauled during that time were horrible loaders. I don't know if it was because the training techniques were worse, or maybe that the 4-H kids loaded their horses so infrequently that they never really had to learn. My Thoroughbred, Roman, loaded himself. I'd just point his nose toward the straight-load narrow stall with the lead rope over his neck and in he would walk, rewarded with hay or grain in the manger. Then I'd fasten the butt strap behind him, fold up the ramp, and off we'd go. Unloading was just as easy. Drop the ramp, undo the butt strap, and pull on the side of his tail to signal him to back out. He was a complete gentleman when it came to loading.

We'd often haul other kids' horses to shows, drill practice, and other events. Few loaded like a gentleman. Many loaded eventually, under duress. Some acted like an untamed mustang. There were a few techniques that seemed to work most of the time, the main one being bribing the horse with grain. Another common technique was to run the lead rope up through the trailer and out the manger window/door, to keep the horse's head directed into the trailer, while having a second very long rope attached to the trailer, going around the horse's butt, and then around the center divider pole. The goal was to pull on both ropes and manhandle (or more often womanhandle) the horse into the trailer. Sometimes it worked.

There was also the long whip method, showing the horse the whip, or tapping the horse with the whip, or finally using it quick and hard on their haunch if they didn't respond to the gentle approach. Sometimes that worked. Loading could take hours of refusals, and trial and error, and repetition.

If there was a cowboy around, especially an old cowboy, there was the "showing the horse who's boss" technique. This often involved chains over the nose, or under the lip, or various combinations. It always worked, although there was a lot of horse pain and worry, and lots of human yelling. Not swearing, because, well, there were kids around.

At some point over the years, loading techniques changed. Loading practice started early with a young horse and it was an expected skill that every horse should know. The natural horsemanship trainers taught us that it was all about moving the feet in response to the step-forward cue. Loading problems are more infrequent now, but they still happen. When it happens, it can still challenge the skills of the best horsewomen.

One of the current techniques is to make the horse more uncomfortable outside of the trailer, than inside. My vet showed me this technique once, when one of my horses didn't load. He had a stick with a plastic bag on it. I pointed the mare into the trailer, while the vet very aggressively shook the bag on the stick, stopping the scary and noisy shaking action only when she stepped in the right direction. With that horse it worked fast.

A few years ago, I joined my neighbor Holly and her friends at the nearby state park. It was just an overnight trip for practice. I had never horse-camped before. I brought Oly, and my son and I camped in our horse trailer. (Brrrr!) There was a day-use equestrian area a half-mile above the horse camping area. Around 10 p.m. that Saturday evening some trail riders appeared out of the dark, horse in hand. They said their truck battery was dead and their horse wouldn't load. When one of our friends couldn't jump-start the truck with their Subaru, I unhooked my truck and brought it up. With the larger truck motor we were able to jump their rig. That was the easy part of the evening.

The horse loading was more of a challenge. They had already been trying for two hours. It was a large, well-lit, 3-horse trailer. We discussed loading their other horse first, however the horses weren't buddies, and they didn't think that would work. Holly tried her favorite technique, of directing the horse's nose into the trailer, and tap-tap-tapping the haunch with the whip until one foot steps in the right direction. Reward by stopping the tapping. Then repeat. In theory, one step at a time, the horse slowly walks into the trailer to get away from the tap-tapping. Holly gave it a good long try, but only got sideways movement from the horse, instead of forward.

I remembered my vet's technique of making a scary situation outside the trailer. I checked the back of my truck for something like a plastic bag and a stick. Nothing. I did have an orange life jacket, though. I grabbed that. I went behind the mare at a safe distance and started shaking that life jacket at arm's length in front of me. She immediately responded with a double-barreled kick straight out, hitting the life jacket square in the middle, and missing me, though completely surprising me with how far and how fast those hind legs flew. I was done with that technique.

We tried tap-tapping some more. Finally, as it got later, we all started to wonder how we would ever get that mare in the trailer. The owner stepped up, calmed the mare down, lined her up in front of the trailer, and lifted one front hoof onto the trailer. Then she went to the mare's head, and pulled the halter to ask her to step the other leg in. After a long pause, the mare moved and stepped both fronts in, and finally just walked in. This was after more than three hours of trying our various methods. It turned out okay, and the folks made it home.

After a long history of loading challenges, I'm so happy every day that my current horses load and unload without drama, and they stay up on all fours when hauling. It makes everything easier. In this instance, I do know how lucky I am.

Devil Trailer

I sold my blue 4-horse stock trailer. I'd had it for eight years and it was old when I bought it. I put some work into it, welding, painting, and wiring. But it was due for more work and I was tired of hitting my head on the under-manger tack area every time I pulled out my saddle.

My next trailer was a 3-horse slant load, old but not ancient, and in solid condition. All the lights worked, and it had a walk-in tack room. Luxury.

In my old stock trailer, I would let my horses turn around before unloading, and walk them forward off the back step. I remember years ago thinking they should learn to back out. I tried once, then my horse said, "No thanks, why should I back when I can just turn around?" I gave up after one try.

My first hauling trip in the new trailer was to a nearby arena for a riding lesson. I loaded Kissi up, pushed her into the angled stall, and pinned the divider into position beside her. She glared at me as if to say, "Where's my old trailer?"

I hauled her to the arena, parked toward the back of the property, and stepped into the trailer to unload her. I pulled the divider to the side, untied Kissi and backed her up a bit, aiming her haunches toward the opening. Kissi stopped, completely on the trailer, back hooves still a half-step from the edge. She would not back up. Coaxing didn't work. Threatening didn't work. I looked around. The new trailer looked about as wide as my old trailer. I thought she might be able to turn around, and at this rate I was going to be late for my lesson. So I let her turn around like we used to do, with me kind of behind her in the trailer, holding the rope, asking her to turn. Surprisingly this trailer was narrower than my old one because of the way the dividers folded back—about 8 inches narrower. My compact medium-sized horse crashed and banged and forced herself around, knocking me off the trailer edge as she jumped out. I rolled a somersault backward in the sand and jumped up to catch my mare before she really embarrassed me. I was fine but looked around to see if anybody had witnessed my skilled gymnastic trailer departure. Luckily no one was watching. I slapped the dust off my clothes and acted as if nothing had happened. Yeah, that's it, my horse got out of the trailer, and everything was fine, and I did not do a backward roll in the dirt.

I tacked Kissi up, rode in my lesson, loaded her back into the trailer and immediately backed her out again for practice. She backed out perfectly. I hauled her home confident we had the problem licked.

At home, she wouldn't back out. I asked my husband for help, tried to back her out, bribed her with grain, hit her, tried to scare her. Nothing doing. She wasn't stepping out backward. I finally let her do the scary crashing turn around inside the trailer again, though this time she didn't knock me over. I was tired. It was dark. We were done.

Over time I worked on this problem. First, I parked the trailer against a rise, so the step-down was shallow. I walked Kissi half-in, and half out, repeating this many times. I rewarded the coming out with grain. Next, we stepped all the way in, then all the way out, and rewarded her with grain. In the pasture I built a ledge against a little hill with two railroad ties. I walked her half up, then down, until that was easy. Eventually I got her going in and backing out of the trailer easily. I moved the trailer so the step was higher. In out, in out. She was doing well! I took her to a lesson. She absolutely refused to back out. After a half-hour, I gave up and let her turn around. I was very tense and frustrated through my lesson. I took her home, parked her in the easy spot with a small step. She refused to back out. I left her in the trailer in 100-degree weather. I tried her every 15 minutes. One-and-a-half hours later, she finally backed out.

I realized that it wasn't that Kissi couldn't back out, it was that she didn't trust me once the trailer was moved to a new location. I could almost hear her little horse brain thinking, *If I have just walked in the trailer, I know how big the step is, and I can back out easy. If the trailer has moved, I don't know how big the step is, and it could be a cliff, and why would I back off a cliff?*

I queried my horsey friends. One said just turn her around. Another said she isn't free in her movements. Do lots of groundwork, get her to back easily on the ground first. A third friend said it is distrust, and to do lots of groundwork and back her over every safe obstacle I can think of.

I ignored the "turn her around" advice, since that wasn't solving my problem, and we began the groundwork. I was a dressage rider. We dressage queens are famous for subtleties and movement from pressure while mounted on the horse. But on the ground, at least in that era, our horses were often spoiled pigs. Or maybe just my horse. She'd as soon knock you over on her way to get a treat as go around you. Her nickname wasn't "Miss Piggy" for nothing. She could really numb out to pressure. It took me a long time to teach her to respond to soft leg cues. It had never occurred to me to teach her to respond to a soft subtle halter or rope cue, rather than simply dragging her along.

I dumped the thick web halter and put on a narrow rope halter. A friend came over to teach me to get her to yield to pressure. The first day I worked with Kissi to go backward my fingers bled from pulling and rubbing the halter on her nose to get a response.

The next day I wore gloves, but Kissi was better. I hardly rode her for a month. We worked on backing, yielding the hip to rope pressure, moving with me, backing between poles, backing over old rugs, side-passing on wood rails, and backing down my homemade ledge. The trailer in and out got better at home. One Sunday afternoon I hauled her around the block. Came home, parked, and she refused to back out again. So I let her stay in. I tried her every 15 minutes. Pressure didn't work. Hitting her chest didn't work. My family went out to dinner without me. I stayed and tried to calmly and gently get my horse out of the trailer. Sometimes less calmly. She completely shut down. She would not move her feet. I finally had the bright idea of stepping on her coronet band right above the hard hoof. One at a time, just to get movement. Finally, by back pressure on the halter and stepping on those feet, and pulling and stepping and pushing and swearing, I got her out of the trailer backward.

I finally found the trick that works when she gets stuck. I have to get her to move just one foot at a time. A stick or long whip tickling her pastern might have worked too.

Since then, my worst unload took five minutes. Eventually she would unload backward as if she'd been doing it forever. This was the beginning of my journey of understanding the importance of groundwork for horses. They have to move their feet.

Backing Trailers

I rode as a teenager, and my mom and my aunt would take me to 4-H, lessons, and to horse shows. My aunt had a trailer, and her boyfriend had an old, white Ford truck. They quickly got tired of hauling me and my horse, though. As soon as I got my driver's license, they were teaching me how to do my own hauling. However, neither my mom nor my aunt was very good at backing a horse trailer. It was kind of a thing, back then, that when you arrived at a horse show or anywhere with tight parking, you looked around for a dad or a farmer to back the trailer in. I never thought twice about it, I just figured backing was hard and took forever to learn. The dads also liked to feel useful during the early morning chaos of a horse show with horses and trailers coming and going. They would back my trailer wherever it needed to be, and in those crowded parking areas I was happy to give them the keys.

It took time to learn to back a trailer confidently. I remember reading in *Western Horseman* magazine about a trick that made all the difference for me. Hold your hand at the bottom of the steering wheel. If you want the back of the trailer to go to the left, move the steering wheel (still holding at the bottom) to the left. And vice versa to back the trailer to the right. With that trick, and a lot of practicing, I became competent at backing horse-trailers. Not stupendous, just competent.

Except for one little thing. I have to be able to see the trailer. If I look out the pickup side window, or over my shoulder, I can back a horse trailer up on a 90-degree turn without too much thought. But if you ask me to back an empty boat trailer down a ramp, and I can't see the trailer over the tailgate, I can jackknife it quicker than a trucker in an ice storm. If my camper is on the back of my truck, and I have to rely on mirrors to back my horse trailer into a spot any smaller than a polo field, I might as well be trying to back the Budweiser Clydesdale team in a serpentine around a line of orange cones during a white-out blizzard.

Another challenge with trailers is backing the truck up to the trailer hitch to hook it up. I used to do this alone, a lot, before the days of rearview video. I would find a center spot on the tail gate and a center spot on the trailer, trying to match those spots while slowly backing. Then I would stop, set the parking brake, and run out and look. Slowly I would get closer and closer. I usually had to get out and check about 47 times during a typical hitching event. But eventually I got it done.

Most of the time now, I ask my husband to help hook up the trailer. This is one of those husband/wife teamwork moments that requires strategic thinking and communication skills. After much experience, I have determined that I would rather be the driver than the director/guider in the trailer-hook-up scenario. In part because the driver can blame the director when the hitch ball is off to the side by an inch. Plus, my husband has good subtle hand symbols, that make sense and communicate the distance to go and the angle to turn. I, on the other hand, wave my arms dramatically and give loud verbal commands that aren't quite yelling, and that usually result in the need to pull forward and try again. Several times. Eventually my husband gets grouchy.

I have found the best technique of all, though, is to leave for work in the morning and tell my husband that I need the trailer hooked up in the evening. When I get home, it's all hooked up, with no yelling or dramatic hand signals necessary.

Now I have the hooking-up-the-trailer scenario solved and can back up the trailer if I can look over my shoulder, however I still need to work on backing with mirrors only. That's going to take some time, thought, and practice. But maybe there's a trick to it that's described in a horse magazine. Off to the bookstore to start my research!

Flood Stage

On the river, that day of the flood, I saw the misstep. That warm spring day we were riding in the park near the river. Flood stage. I was in back as we rode single file, angling down the bluff to see the flooding river up close. I don't like heights or edges, so my horse was in back where I had room to move and breathe. Rene rode in front with her big, experienced trail horse, then came Mimi, each with a daughter on a horse between us, with me in back because I don't like rivers at flood stage. I watched from above: Rene's horse, the first horse, followed the trail down to where it flattened and the river came over the trail, the water calm at the edge of the flood in the trees. I watched the horse stop, drop his head to drink, and take one step further. I watched that horse step off the trail and fall forward into a soft nothing where the edge had become wet silt. Rene pushed back, off the horse, out of the saddle backward into the water. She was loose and still falling back into the shallows of the eddy while the horse fell forward, swimming now in the main channel of the flooding river.

Where will we find him? I think, watching him swim away beside the flooded trees, nose downstream, swimming with the current. *How will we call for help?* I wonder, stepping out of my saddle. *Where are we exactly?*

I tell the girls to hold my horse and theirs. Mimi's down at the edge off her horse and we're all watching Rene's horse swim. *Can Rene swim? Her daughter's watching this.* Watching Rene stand up thigh deep, watching Rene's horse as he turned, swimming back across the current toward the trail where it used to be, watching him climb onto where the bank used to be, into the shallows, into the trees, somehow getting out of the channel downstream, and walking through the flooded forest. Rene walking out toward him, away from us with no hesitation, into the flood, water over her knees and standing on who knows what is left underneath.

Too many legs are in that river, even at that calm spot in the trees. I went in over my good riding boots, to try to help, yet not knowing how to help, not going further. Nothing to do but watch. Watching Rene's horse come toward her call, watching Rene catch her horse, too close to the roiling current for me, wet over my knees. Rene walking back, full-body wet, with her horse at her side.

We all lived that spring day tempting the flood, dumping frigid water out of boots, giving Rene a dry raincoat from the back of my saddle for warmth, riding an hour back to her house. All those legs in danger, all those legs walking out safe. No cold, no fear, just adrenalin. All night I saw that horse fall forward in the river, Rene leaping off backward. Leap after leap, time after time.

Searching for a Unicorn

I have come to believe there's no such thing as a beginner's horse, that bomb-proof creature of myth, that plods down the trail and doesn't shy from semi-trucks, motorcycles, black bears, or helicopters landing in front of his nose. The baby-sitter horse that you can put anybody on. I have heard of these all-knowing beings, I may even have met one, possibly two in my life as a horseman, but they are as rare as a unicorn. When I've been looking for that extra do-everything, put-anybody-on-it horse, I've never found it. Even in the ads today, if I looked, the only beginner horses would come in the too-old-and-sore-to-be-bad version. Too sore on its feet to run away.

Maybe I don't really want my extra horse to be a beginner's horse. Then I have to put up with beginner riders, and it takes a lot of energy to be always teaching, lecturing, guiding that naïve new rider to avoid death or major injury. But still, it would be nice to have a horse where I could just give a friend a leg-up and hit the dusty trail. Maybe I'm looking in the wrong place. There must be online classified ads that sell mythical beasts. Surely a beginner-safe horse can be found somewhere in between the Centaur and Pegasus ads.

Classified Ads: Green Broke Horse, Ready to Go in Any Direction

I love reading classified advertisements for horses. In this era of internet, Craigslist, and Facebook, I can imagine buying several horses over a 15-minute web-surfing break at work. Between my adventures buying my own horses over the years, helping friends buy horses, and just generally watching the ads, I believe I have developed an understanding of the language of horse ads. It's not plain English. There are cultural meanings, regional meanings, and just plain lies associated with the verbiage in a typical horse ad. Sometimes it's like a used car salesman wrote the ad and embellished a lot: "This horse has low miles and was only used by an old lady to ride to church on Sundays." Other times it's just that the writer really doesn't know what she's talking about and is trying to get rid of a horse that was too much for her from the start. Rarely do you find an ad that's honest, where the owner is clearly trying to find a good home for a decent horse.

Whether I'm seriously looking for a horse, or just on an imaginary search, I love to look online. I can check key sales websites or Facebook listings multiple times a day. I can look locally, or I can search the whole Northwest, or nationwide. On some websites I can search by breed, age, gender, or other details. It's an addiction. It's an addiction to imagination. I imagine each horse living at my house, getting to know my family, and going on long lovely trail rides without either of us falling off a cliff. I imagine taking up new riding disciplines just because I like the picture of a trained endurance horse, or a draft horse team. Everything is good in these fictional horse relationships. There are no surprise training issues, no health problems or hidden lameness, and the sun shines every day.

With all this practice reading horse ads, I have learned many of the hidden codes. I will share them with you, though recognize that there may still be more to learn. The jargon continually evolves, and there may be subtleties within certain breeds or disciplines that I will never truly understand. The following defines some of the secret terms as I know them today:

Experienced rider only.

Translation: This horse is an idiot and needs complete retraining. Let's note here that I am probably considered an experienced rider, though I'm not a professional trainer or anywhere near it. But in my experience, and at my age, it's nice to have a mellow and well-trained horse, and not to have to fix ingrained training issues or fight a runaway for the whole ride. Who has that kind of energy, or time, except maybe teenage horse-loving girls, and/or professional trainers that get paid to fix those troublesome horses? For those of you who are in this group, please wear a helmet.

Needs confident rider.

Translation: This is a pushy horse, don't ever turn your back. It's unpredictable, stubborn, and poorly trained. This horse should never be bought for a beginner or a small child even if it's the color or breed or type they always wanted. Personally, I'm too lazy to be that alert all the time.

Horse is looking for a job.

Translation: Horse was fired from last job as a family horse and is now looking for a new sucker, I mean owner. This reminds me of some co-workers I prefer not to spend time with. If you don't ride the horse every day and work off the excess energy, it's unpredictable.

Horse is a free spirit.

Translation: I have no idea what this phrase means, yet it's intriguing. Untrained and does what it wants? Reads cowboy poetry and prefers its grass smoked and in zigzag papers?

Needs finishing.

Translation: Walks, trots, canters, but stops are iffy, and it doesn't steer worth a darn. Not enough time in my busy life to fix those problems.

Kid's horse, or dead broke.

Translation: Too old to be rambunctious. Near dead and will break your kid's heart.

Very Athletic.
Translation: Bucks really well.

Green broke, or needs more training.
Translation: Not broke at all but had a saddle on. Once.

Green broke horse, ready to go in any direction.
Translation: This could be a heck of a deal, if the horse is truly broke and just inexperienced. This could be the horse that you get young, and then turn it into the mount you always wanted. Or, it could be pretty much un-broke, and been handled and saddled but not trained to move. This would be the instance when "ready to go in any direction" could mean any direction the horse wants, including straight up.

Had 30 days professional training (or 60 days or 90 days).
Translation: Was trained once long ago and has since forgotten everything she knew. This label is often used for brood mares that were trained as 3-year-olds, then used to pop out a decade or two of babies. Now, past the breeding age, they are attempting to sell her as a trained riding horse. Too much work.

Never had professional training.
Translation: Ask questions, and, depending on the answers, consider going to look. My best horses have been trained by teenage girls in 4-H or Pony Club. Some teenage girls have passion, skill, and most of all, time, for training and riding and putting hours on a horse. It is hours under a decent rider that makes the horse, not the first 30 days of professional training. Of course, it might also mean the horse doesn't stop or steer, and it only follows other horses.

Herd reduction sale.
Translation: The farm owner saw the light. There's no money in horses. He's trying to sell the breeding stock before he needs to buy more hay in the fall, while still trying to get a high price out of these stunning show horses with stupendous breeding lines (that he never had the time to train or show).

Has great breeding.

Translation: These ads always include a long list of famous (at least locally) sires, dams, grand-sires, grand-dams, and distant cousins who once won some money in a reining class or a horse race. The more information provided on breeding lines, the less information provided on temperament, training, or health. As a good friend once said, "You can't ride the papers."

Good in saddle, but ground manners stink.

Translation: Self-explanatory. Don't buy her. Undoubtedly bad in saddle, too; she just can't bite or kick you as easily.

Free horse, has seeing problem.

Translation: At least this person is honest about a serious health problem. But beware the *24-year-old, bomb-proof, dead-broke kid's horse.* This is my pet peeve. If you have a really old horse, and you can afford it, try to let him live out his years at your house. If you can't, don't expect a lot of money from him. It can be a kindness to put him down. I can only speak for myself, but I'm not going to buy your old horse and watch it go lame and pay your vet bills. I already have my own long-time family member horses to do that with.

Rescue horse at kill pen.

Translation: If you think that it's hard to figure out a horse based on a classified ad, try figuring out a horse that's in an auction yard. You know nothing. You see a tear-jerker picture, and an assessment from the yard watcher on the quality of this horse based on a bareback ride and its attitude. There are stories of those horses becoming famous jumping horses, although more often you hear stories of ending up with a sick or unrideable money pit. More power to people who use their horse passion to save a horse at the kill pen, but these are not always happy endings, and you should go in fully aware.

A few years ago, after relearning the lingo of horse ads, I started looking for a new horse for myself. Not only did I want an experienced trail horse that can pack, that's suitable for beginners so my kids could ride, and is kind and mellow, I really wanted a short horse. A large pony or small horse. It just seemed logical that for my goal of riding and packing in the mountains short would be an advantage. Short, kind, and with strong legs and hooves. And sound. And bomb proof. That's all I wanted, and, of course, for a reasonable price. Surely, I could find such an animal. Eventually.

I went to see one large stocky black pony, supposedly a good trail horse, according to the ad. She was cute, however she tensed up when you sat on her and she didn't steer so well. Needs more training.

I visited a sorrel quarter-pony. She was cute but "cinchy." She jumped and hunched up when cinching the saddle and looked ready to explode. She was nice to ride. On the other hand, messing with a cinchy horse on a cold morning in the wilderness seemed like a lot of effort. Too many issues.

I went to look at a Fjord Horse with no professional training, and good for beginners, according to the ad. I'd always wanted a Fjord Horse. I fell in love with the mare, and the breed, even before the test ride. I was planning to buy her after the initial tacking up. Then I got on her and rode down the trail. She was lame. Such a bummer. Even if it was just a muscle pull from a trail ride the day before, it seemed unwise to buy a horse for mountain riding that injured easily. She was moderately expensive, it was tax season, and I owed taxes. Not a good month to buy a horse.

Eventually I did find my short-stocky, calm horse with lots of trail experience. I looked at Oly and his pasture mate, Jeb. Both were Fjord Horses. Both were chubby from too much rich spring grass. Jeb was older and had really long unhealthy hooves. Oly walked, trotted, cantered, steered, and stopped. The owner's friend, an experienced rider, said, "He'll be great after a few hours of tuning up." I can tune up a horse, I thought. After all of those years of riding lessons, how hard can it be? Oly joined our family.

Oly. Photo credit Cindy Miller.

Oly and the Barrels

Maybe buying Oly the Norwegian Fjord Horse wasn't the bravest thing I've ever done. I wondered for a while whether buying him might have been the stupidest thing I've ever done. Later, on the good days, I thought buying him might have been the most fun thing I've ever done.

It was mid-life crisis time. My kids were getting older, I had a bit more time to myself, and my two older Appaloosas were retired, basically expensive pasture pets. I needed a horse to ride. Not just any breed. I wanted a trail horse and a mountain horse. A short horse seemed to be an advantage when riding through trees.

Fjord Horses have unique coloring, with the most common color being a brown dun (similar to a buckskin). They have a dark or black stripe in the middle of their mane, and the stripe usually continues down their back and into their tail. This makes their mane and tail a symmetrical two-tone with white on the outside and darker or black in the middle. They have an intelligent face and big eyes, and darker stripes or mottling on their legs. They look like a cross between a zebra and a draft horse, and they are noted for their calm character.

Two Fjord Horses were for sale an hour north of our house. I test-rode Oly, the younger horse of the two, in his pasture. He walked, trotted, and cantered. He definitely wasn't fine-tuned, nevertheless I was sure I could improve him. I made a deal and took him home. It was only later that I remembered his previous owner mentioning that Oly was the more stubborn of the two.

My first few rides on the property and around the neighborhood were not great. Oly danced and pranced a lot. He was not the lazy, calm horse I expected. He was barn sour, always wanting to head back toward home. I'm a good rider and have ridden for years, however I'm not a skilled trainer. I've been able to improve horses over time but have never trained from scratch. With Oly I thought I would just ride consistently, and we would figure each other out and in time he would be great. He wasn't really bad, but he wasn't really good either. Except when I was leading him, then he was calm and would follow me anywhere.

A few weeks after I got Oly, I met some friends with their horses in the local state park to ride on the trails. I wanted to see how Oly acted on the trails in a new place. After unloading him from the trailer he was very nervous. I saddled him and walked him around, and he stayed tense. My friends arrived, and saddled up, and Oly was still worried and sweating. I mounted anyway, and rode him in line behind the other horses, and was pleased to learn that Oly was a follower. He walked down the trail fairly well. But I also soon realized I had very little control. He wanted to be on the other horse's tail. That's a dangerous place. He was very focused on the other horses in our group and was oblivious to me. He was an accident waiting to happen.

At one point the two teenager riders in the group moved off to ride their horses fast up a hill, and two of us stayed behind. Oly was frantic that part of his herd was leaving; he wanted to follow them. I tightened the reins to tell him no, stay with this horse here. He answered my request by leaping forward and showing me he was stronger, and could go where he wanted. I pulled him back again and he kept hopping. I did the horseman's emergency move: I pulled hard on one rein to do little circles, to occupy him and keep him in a small space and keep us both safe. He turned his head in response to the rein, while his body kept going the way of the other horses. At that point we were on the side of the road and a car was coming. The other horse next to me was having his own arguments with his rider. I really had no control of my sideways-moving horse that couldn't see where he was going. I didn't fall off, and the car slowed and didn't hit us. Still, that situation was dangerous. It wasn't long before the other horses came back, and everyone settled down and walked calmly again, even Oly, although it was on his terms, not mine. That's when I again remembered his previous owner saying he was the stubborn one. I also remembered she did not seem to be a skilled horsewoman. I was starting to wonder what sort of spoiled pony I had, and how hard it would be to get past that trait. It was going to take some real training, and I was going to need help. Those long mountain trail rides would have to wait.

Oly and I continued to have challenges. We had a few good rides, but on the bad days, he would buck, spin, and bolt toward home. I'm a balanced rider, and he's a poor bucker, so I didn't fall off during those out-of-control moments. Once he did that buck/run move, even after I stopped him, he would be buzzed and hyper and every little thing would scare him. He would forget how to walk. Again, I had little control. I queried other Fjord owners online. This testing of limits and trying to be the boss was typical of the breed. Plus, it's easy to let a cute little teddy bear of a horse get away with a lot. I knew I couldn't let Oly be the leader however I wasn't sure how to show him I was the boss.

I found a trainer. Oly and I went to three different multi-day clinics with Ann. Ann was a natural horsemanship type trainer, where rather than fighting a war with the horse and wearing it out until it submits, she taught us how to assert dominance on the horse's terms, as if you were the boss horse in the herd. There's a lot of skill and subtlety and watching of body postures to determine how the horse is responding. There's a gradual building on each step until the horse is responding to you and your body language and you truly become the boss mare in the relationship.

Ann spent a lot of time on groundwork. Her goal was to get the horse through its issues while you weren't on its back. With Ann's help, I would ask Oly to do a task, like stop when I stop, and if he didn't respond correctly, she would teach me how to get the correct answer. He must always do what I want when I want, or at least make a move toward the right answer. It was like starting him over from scratch. I don't think I taught him everything, but the process helped him to be calm so that he could remember what he once knew, focus on what I was asking, and learn new stuff.

Ann was all about safe trail riding. As we worked our horses on the ground, she asked us to maneuver over simple objects such as we might see on a trail. Orange cones are like maneuvering through trees, a sheet might be a vine hanging from a branch, a tarp is like water to walk over, and two blue barrels laid on their sides end to end are like a very big log. Oly was a star going over and through the obstacles. If he was calm to start with, the obstacles did not bother him. Except for the blue barrels. At the first two training clinics, we didn't even try the barrels. Oly is short legged, and those barrels came up almost to his belly. I watched the other riders coax their long-legged horses over the barrels from the ground, standing beside them and guiding them forward with the rein in one hand, and whip pointed toward their haunch with the other hand. With this technique they attempted to drive their horses forward from the ground. I watched their hesitations as their horses lined up, thought about stepping over, moved one leg up and over, changed their mind, backed off, tried again, readjusted, then finally hopped over to big praise from their owners. I was sure Oly couldn't jump that high from a standstill and I avoided that obstacle.

Toward the end of our third clinic, Ann pushed us to try the barrels. She showed me how to line Oly up, how to hold the rein so his choice was to stand, or go over the barrel with no other options. She showed me how to reward him for each movement in the right direction, even if it's just a posture change or a tiny step forward. Ann taught me how to wait for a positive response, and how to tap him again to move him forward. Oly thought about those blue barrels and stood, moved a bit, thought some more, then used all his strength to say *no* and leave that obstacle. With the arena fence on one side, and me on the other, his way out was pushing through me. Absolutely not, I would tell him with quick discipline and pulling on the rein. I would line him up to try again. He would think about it, start to step over, change his mind, and blow past me again and again. Oly might be short, but he's solid, and I was a movable object.

Ann watched Oly buffalo me again, then took the reins. She more adamantly told him with her voice and body language to stand there and don't crowd her. She guided him to face the barrels directly. She cued him to go over, and when he started his move to crowd Ann, she made her small body big and popped him with the whip as if she were a boss mare telling a lowly pasture mate to back off. In the face of Ann's insistence, Oly finally went over those blue barrels. Jumping easily from a standstill. But I was done and was still intimidated by those barrels.

That last clinic was in the fall, and through the winter Oly and I worked on listening to the rein cues and going over obstacles. I built a bridge; he walked over it on the first try. I hung fake "vines" between two trees; he walked through them like they were nothing. We carried a long branch from one place to another and it was as if he'd been doing it forever. We dragged feed bags full of clanging cans. No problem.

Early the next spring I laid two barrels on their sides, end to end, next to a fence. I lined him up, with the rein in one hand and the whip in the other hand and guided him to face the barrels. I tapped him forward. The first time he pushed toward me I yelled and hit him hard like a boss mare teaching manners to her foal. He looked at me like I was possessed and backed away in surprise. I lined him up again, directing him forward. He chewed on the bit a moment, thinking, then sat back on his haunches and hopped over those barrels like he'd been doing jumper courses his whole life. Cleared them. From a standstill. He did it again without hesitation from the other direction. Days later we practiced again, and again he went over without hesitation. Oly did what I asked, and together we conquered those intimidating barrels.

I can't explain why the barrels made the difference. It was our turning point. Since then, Oly has tested me once in a while, but he quickly gave it up and listened. He calmed down quickly after shying from things and he stopped bucking and bolting. We began learning to canter more smoothly and calmly. Oly was fun to ride! All I had to do was embrace my inner boss-mare. Now, how do I do this at work with my coworkers . . .

My Mid-Life Crisis Is Better than Yours

My husband tells me his new/used boat is *not* a mid-life crisis, he doesn't need a mid-life crisis, and he's not going to have a mid-life crisis. But I'm his wife and I helped him pick out the boat for his mid-life crisis, so I proclaim it a mid-life crisis. I, on the other hand, bought Oly the Norwegian Fjord Horse as my mid-life crisis. My horse is obviously better than Doug's boat, as far as mid-life crises go. My comparison follows:

The Boat	Oly the Fjord Horse
The boat can hold 5 people.	Oly can carry lunch for 5 people.
The motor needs a tune-up.	Oly's training needs a tune-up.
If the motor breaks, you're stuck in the middle of the lake.	If Oly bucks me off and runs away, I can still walk home.
We can fish lakes with the boat.	We can fish mountain streams with Oly to carry our gear.
The boat likes water, and when running fast, it makes a big wake.	Oly likes water and makes a wake in ponds with his nose.
The boat floats like a cork.	Oly eats like a moose (nose underwater grabbing succulent grass).
The boat goes where Doug steers.	Oly walks where I lead.
The boat runs on gas.	Oly runs on hay and sometimes has gas.
The boat makes Doug smile.	Oly makes me smile.
The boat needs new gear.	Oly needs all new tack.
The boat has a wide beam.	Oly is also wide in the beam.
The boat is sleek and streamlined.	Oly is short and stocky.
The boat parks in the garage all winter.	Oly needs his stall cleaned.
The boat likes salt water.	Oly would probably buck and run on the beach.

The boat only likes mountains as something to be hauled across on the way to the ocean.	Oly thinks mountains are for walking up.
The boat came with a motor.	Oly came with a halter.
The boat has nice lines.	Oly looks like a teddy bear.
The boat has a shallow V hull.	Oly has a draft-horse belly.
If you don't like boats, you won't like this boat either.	If you don't like horses, you'll like this one.
A Viking would like this boat.	A Viking would like this horse.

They both need a big truck and trailer for hauling.

Journal: Oly, Spring

May 2012

Yesterday my mom let the horses out to graze. First the old gelding Kodo, (always the boss), walked out into our seasonal pond to eat little green tips of tender grass. Next my mare Kissi (always the grouch) walked out into the pond beside Kodo to nibble on the grass. Finally, Oly, who always gets picked on by Kissi, looked out at the pond and the calmly grazing horses, got a horse-smirk on his face, and proceeded to canter through the shallow pond close to Kissi's head, splashing water all over her face. Then he turned around and did it again. Eventually he got tired of splashing Kissi and settled down to graze on the sweet, green grass. Soon, Kissi casually and quietly walked over to Oly, and bit him in the rear end. My mom has coined new names for the horses: The Boss, The B-word (Bother?), and The Brat.

June 2012

Oly's been good recently, really good. But he's such an imp! He'll throw a surprise at you, just to see if he can get away with something. His tricks keep changing. Like riding home from my neighbor's property. It had been a great ride, alone, through woods, up, down, and over rough rocks. Even going home he was calmly walking on a loose rein, until, as he got closer to the last turn toward home he suddenly jumped into a canter. I swear he faked a shy! There was nothing spooky around, no wind, no cars, dogs, or fluttering paper—he completely made it up. I immediately pulled one rein, he stopped nicely and disengaged the hip (a partial turn on the forehand). I turned him around and walked him back to my neighbor's driveway, turned him back to do the same stretch again, and he walked calmly yet energetically, on a loose rein. However, when I cued him to continue past our driveway rather than tuning into it, he walked as slow as he possibly could, barely continuing forward motion. Way down the road, Oly saw a neighbor walking toward us. Oly stopped, as if to say, *Oh my gosh what's that weird creature way up there? I must stop and snort at it! Oh, it's just a human.* I coaxed him on. Then he seemed to say, *But wait, back behind us by the hill two yellow creatures are coasting without legs! I can't go forward; they might eat me! Oh, it's just bicycles.* Since he had now gotten away with two successful stops because he "might be scared," he decided he no longer needed to go forward at all. Standing was fine for him but heading away from home was not. I nudged him with my heels. Nothing. I kicked him four times. Nada. Finally, I pulled my lead rope off my saddle horn and popped him on his hip. He moved right out, though clearly was disgusted as if saying, *Oh, you mean 'walk!' Well, shoot, why didn't you say so?* Now I'm waiting for his next trick, which will surely be different than the last one.

Life Is Short

Kodo was the horse I always wanted as a teenager. He was calm, with no vices, well trained, and would do anything I asked. We rode dressage and bareback, went trail riding, and jumping. I could ride him with a halter and lead rope, or even just a neck rope. He would "listen" to that simple rope and move away from the pressure. He was gentle and little kids could feed him by hand. He was quiet enough to lead him with kids on his back. When I had kids of my own, I could ride with them in front of me. Kodo would pull the kids on a sled in the winter. Later as my boys got older, he was the lesson horse. My advanced horse friends could ride Kodo and my beginner friends could ride him. My 70-year-old aunt rode him and loved him. He was the perfect family horse.

Plus, Kodo was gorgeous. He was always shiny with dapples in the summer and unlike most Appaloosas, he had a long, thick and wavy mane and tail. He did inherit the Appaloosa mindset, though. He was obedient, yet stubborn. Kodo was clever and had lips as agile as a hand with an opposable thumb. When I tied my mare at the corner post by Kodo's pen, he would untie her lead rope, or unbuckle her halter, so she could escape to graze in the yard. Kodo would untie his own lead rope, and if that didn't work, he would grab the rope loop with his teeth, and try to toss it over the top of the corner post. He was often successful. Kodo could also undo stall latches. I had to use three latches on his stall door, with an extra clip for security. If I was in a hurry and only latched one, he would escape in no time.

Kodo was playful. He would reach anything he could outside his stall door and toss it. He would pull halters off their hooks, toss brushes off the bench, and play with buckets or rakes. One time my son saw him reach the wheelbarrow handle, tip it over, grab it again, pull it towards him, and tip it over again. Nothing was safe anywhere near the stall.

He was also the only horse I knew that would see us with the hose on a hot summer day and come up and ask for a shower. He would walk up to the fence, toss his head, and then walk into the spray we directed toward him, turning around until both sides of his neck and body were wet and cool. Or he would wait at the edge of his paddock for the yard sprinkler to rotate his direction and stand under it. He was totally into comfort. He taught me to find all his itchy spots by pointing with his nose and moving until I got the right spot. One spot inside his thigh would cause him to raise his rear leg like a dog and wiggle his lips with delight. Anyone watching would think I was about to be kicked.

Kodo was almost four when I got him. At fourteen, he started limping intermittently. He developed arthritis early. He was partially retired to be a trail and guest horse. Eventually, as the arthritis hit more joints and became worse, he became a pasture pet.

At 26, an odd wound appeared above one rear hoof. It turned out to be a melanoma tumor, a type of skin cancer. Kodo was in severe pain. That kind horse who never bit or kicked a human in his life, would try to kick me when I changed the bandage. After exploring invasive and iffy treatment options, we had our vet put him down. The week before he got lots of treats and attention. It was a rough week for me, saying goodbye to my long-time friend and family member, yet it was clearly the right decision. The night before, our whole family raised our glasses to Kodo: a toast to the best horse ever and the best kodo (money) I ever spent.

All the Things I Do Wrong

All the things I do wrong, my trainer can see.
To her it's black or it's white, it's hard or it's soft,
There is no gray, my favorite shade in the world of horses.
If it's not right, do it again
And again. Fifty more times. Five hundred.
The answer is only right if it's correct every time,
Good enough's not acceptable
Even more so with my draft pony: all muscle and opinion.
Give him an inch, he'll take you to the moon!
Three days of learning and practicing, till the sweat rolls off his solid sides.
Assignments and homework, I jot little notes on yellow paper,
Maybe I can remember the steps to teach my tug-of-war horse
To be soft, like caramel, the color of his coat on a summer day.

Saddle Shopping

I was riding English, now I plan to hit the trails.
I don't have to change saddles, but I like those stringy tails—
Latigos, they call them; and then there's the horn,
That handy little handle, when there's a bucking storm.

I do have a Western saddle; it fits me like a dream;
My legs hang where they should, but it doesn't fit my steed.
It rises where he drops, it straightens where he curves,
Could be why he bucks, maybe pinching on his nerves.

Since I'm off to buy a saddle, I've asked for some advice.
I've gotten lots of wisdom, but don't know which parts are right:
I should buy a McCall or a Courts, if I don't mind going poor,
Avoid a flex tree or a treeless, or my horse's back will sore.

Get a Colorado draft saddle to fit my wide-backed Fjord,
Maybe an endurance saddle, but then I'd lose that handy horn.
A gaited saddle is sure to fit, it's wide for muscly shoulders.
A balanced ride, a barrel saddle, or maybe try a roper.

I need a quarter horse tree, or Wade tree, of steel, fiberglass, or wood.
An old handmade cowboy saddle might fit, they say it really should.
But the leather shouldn't be too old, or too cheap, or too new.
Maybe synthetic will work, no oiling, and it's waterproof.

The skirt should be round, not square, to fit my short-backed draft.
If only I'd bought a quarter horse, this wouldn't be such a task.
I measured his back at twenty-three, give or take an inch.
The girth should fit forward, back, or middle, or in Western is it a cinch?

The seat should fit the bottom of me, maybe fifteen inches,
Unless somewhat shorter, or longer depending on my preference.
And the stirrups set for balance, with a turn to help my knees.
I need a little comfort, too, for those long rides through the trees.

This saddle's gonna cost me, or maybe not so much.
It depends on where I find it. It depends upon my luck.
But when buying and selling saddles, my luck usually goes.
I have a saddle-shopping motto: buy high and sell low.

Last week I visited our local handmade saddle store,
They carry only working saddles, leather things and more.
The saddler looked at my horse's photos and he started to laugh.
"Maybe four percent of the saddles out there will fit that curvy back."

I headed up north to another place with lots of saddles for sale.
A barn full of saddles stacked three high for showing, barrels, and trail.
Out of 70 saddles in the place only three looked appropriately wide:
An Arab saddle, a synthetic wide-tree, and a draft horse saddle to try.

I wrote out a check and took all three home for a 24-hour test ride.
The draft fit Oly, though the giant slick seat had me sliding side to side.
The synthetic fit me well, and fit my horse sort of just okay.
And the Arab saddle fit neither of us, truly the worst of that day.

I kept the cheap synthetic and returned the other two.
It was better than my old Tex Tan that fit Oly all askew.
It was an imperfect solution, hopefully a temporary fix,
A placeholder until I could find the perfect saddle that fits.

I went to the 4-H tack swap, just looking, not to buy.
Out of a hundred saddles there, only one might fit my guy.
The leather was old yet strong, it was basically real well made.
If I took it home and it didn't work, I could always re-sell on Ebay.

I took home the no-name saddle with the wide flared tree,
I doubtfully put it on Oly's back and cinched it up to see.
It widened where he was muscley and curved up where it should.
It fit his back like a glove, like I never thought it would.

I finally found a saddle that fits both me and my chunky horse.
And still I have the synthetic one, an extra saddle, of course.
All total I have six saddles, for only two horses that ride.
My saddle-to-riding-horse ratio must be getting close to right.

But I still need a pack saddle for my solid little draft.
I have just one little question, although I hesitate to ask . . .
For anyone out there who's packed in with horses overnight,
Do you have any pack saddle purchasing advice?

The Horse in the Mirror

We were riding in the state park, coming down off the old railroad bed, and looking for the connector trail that is a shortcut between that end of the park and Deep Creek, to circle back home. Off through the trees we saw two riders, one on a bay horse, one on a caramel-colored horse. Carol and I angled our horses toward the strangers to say, "Hi." They angled toward us. I saw it before Oly, that caramel-colored horse was a Fjord. But then Oly saw it and his walk quickened. When we were about 30 feet away, he made a beeline to that horse, nickering.

I never let new horses sniff noses. They tend to forget the rider and go all horse-social with squealing, pawing, and biting. They play their submission and dominance games with posturing that can turn aggressive and dangerous for the riders. But this time Oly continued his speed walk right up to that new horse, totally ignoring the bay, totally ignoring my slow-down cues, and sniffed noses with that other Fjord. I let him get away with it this time. There was a tiny squeal and a stomp, then they just stood and breathed each other's breath for long minutes.

The other Fjord was a little shorter and had a longer nose than Oly. Smiling, I asked the rider where the horse came from. "Stehekin," she said. Stehekin is a remote village at the end of Lake Chelan where a family breeds Fjords and uses them for wilderness riding and packing. Our horses kept sniffing. Carol and the other rider talked about horses and trails. The Fjords continued breathing, nostril to nostril, sharing air.

What were they thinking? I'll bet Oly thought it was an old friend, or maybe a cousin. Maybe they are like dog breeds, and really only "get" the same or similar breeds. I had a border collie/Australian shepherd once. While she liked other dogs, she only played hard with similar herding breeds. It was like they were the only ones that knew the right rules to the chase game. Maybe that's what Oly saw—a soul mate that knew the rules to the Fjord Horse games.

Eventually, after mutually admiring each other's horses, which is required when meeting other riders on the trail, we pulled apart and went our separate ways. Oly seemed sated. He didn't look back. I still smile at the picture of him aiming straight toward the horse that looked just like him, straight toward a mirror in the woods.

The Good, the Bad, and the Lucky

It was to be the summer where I finally got into the backcountry with horses. I had an elderly Fjord Horse, and after four years of work, he was becoming a heck of a riding horse. In February I had bought a young green Fjord Horse that I planned to use as a pack horse. He was mentally young, but after a summer of being ponied by the old brave guy, Oly, I was confident he would also be ready for the mountains.

Then Oly went lame. While we addressed the lameness, I started seriously riding the green youngster. This young teenager (mental teenager, not *in* his teens) was a lot different than Oly. Oly is a medium draft-type Fjord. Thick in body, he would prefer to plod along and grab grass rather than expend a lot of energy. Oly is super brave. The only object I found that he really didn't like was sprinklers. Since there aren't many sprinklers in the wilderness, I was sure we were ready for some back country jaunts that year.

The new guy was a different story. First off, when I bought him, his name was all wrong. He didn't have a Norwegian name. His registered name was Abbra's Comanche. Really? That totally sounds like an Appaloosa name. I let my son and husband give him a nickname. They settled on Vali, a Norse god, a son of Odin. But in reality, his name should have been Goofball. He was a total troublemaker. He was not placid and brave like Oly. He was a sportier build, energetic, and only sometimes brave. He was always aware of everything, and truly got nervous in new situations. Vali was always sure he was right and didn't immediately listen to his human. I figured he just needed miles and exposure.

In August, my riding buddy Carol invited me to join a horse-camping group at Calispell Meadows, in the mountains of Northeastern Washington. I was all over it; yes, I would go! Except I remembered that Oly was lame. Hmmm . . . well, it should be fine with Vali. AKA Goofball. AKA Unpredictable. But so far, all five trail rides I had been on with Vali had been fine. I was sure it would be okay.

It started out great. We headed down the trail from the horse camp, just Carol and I. Every time Vali tossed his head, and said let's go, I sat down on him and said, let's walk. And he walked. It was great for the first hour. The trails were lovely, my young horse was silly though obedient. Later, on a narrower trail, with Vali behind and Carol's horse ahead, he felt different. We opted to turn around and move to an open area, where I could do lots of walking and turning and get Vali's brain engaged again. Then we headed back to camp on a dirt road. I thought a trot would settle him. When Carol's horse trotted off ahead, I asked Vali to trot. All I remember was Vali's head curling down and I was on the ground. I am still not sure what he did, but man, that young horse is very athletic, energetic, and can buck. You know how sometimes, you can feel you are going to fall off, you feel it coming, and it is like slow-motion while you pick the spot of dirt you will land in? This was not one of those times. I was on and I was off. Fast, with no in-between. And for those of you that don't know me, I am a pretty decent rider. I don't come off easily. For those of you who don't know my young goofball horse (insert any other phrase you prefer) . . . man, he has some moves.

But the lucky part? I was wearing a helmet. I hit hard, but there were no rocks to make things worse. I was bruised, but not broken. My pride was hurt, but nothing permanent. I lost my water bottle, but it was old and needed replacing. All in all, not a bad result for a bad fall. Plus, I had remembered to pack a flask of whisky in my camping gear.

While healing, I spent time working Vali on the ground. He was good, and I hoped that bucking event was just a fluke on the journey to becoming a solid trail horse. In the meantime, the old guy Oly had been to the vet, and an injection of steroid and joint fluid deep into the front hoof joints helped his lameness. I had my old horse back, at least for the short-term. Now, if only I could do a mind-meld from the old guy to the young guy. I figured within a year Vali would become a good horse and we would get to the back country. I was sure of it.

Michelle on Vali, before the fall. Near Chewelah, Washington.
Photo credit Carol Klar.

Hot Cocoa Snow

Those of us who are outside in all weather, especially during the worst winter weather, have developed words and phrases to describe the types of snow. I don't just mean the long list of swear words and curses to use while shoveling gates open, thawing water pipes, or after spilling several bucket sloshes onto your jeans in the dark when it's 23 degrees out in order to fill the trough just deep enough to make it until you get home from work. Beyond those unprintable phrases, I have started a vocabulary of horse people's snow. Okay, there are only seven terms so far, however winter is coming. I'm sure I can find more.

1) Pasture Snow.

This is snow that has a texture that makes you want to leave the horse in the pasture, paddock, or stall. Riding is dangerous due to slick or deep conditions. Pasture snow can be deceptive—it may look fluffy and fun, however it hides buried ice from the last two weeks of rain, thaw, rain, freeze cycles before it was covered with snow. You know it's pasture snow when you can barely make it to the barn on two legs—and you give thanks that at least the horses have four legs to help hold them up.

2) Riding Snow.

My favorite riding snow is soft and fluffy powder, about four inches deep, with day-time highs of about 31 degrees, and no wind. The snow cushions the gravel road in front of our house, it causes grown-ups to act like kids, and horses to act like colts. This snow just begs for jingle bells to be tied to the saddle. Riding snow is best after a dry period—to minimize potential for hidden ice (see Pasture Snow).

3) Deep Riding Snow.

More than four inches with no lurking ice. I keep the rides short, because the deep snow tires the horse, however the riding is delightful. Perfect for schooling your horse in passage (a slow, high stepping, dressage trot).

4) Abrasive Snow.

Deep riding snow can turn to abrasive snow. Freezing rain or a one-day thaw of deep snow causes a crust on the top. One year we had a foot of snow, followed by freezing rain. I couldn't figure out why my horse was slow and hesitant to ride. He usually loved snow! After the ride when I was walking through the pasture in the knee-deep snow, I found the problem. The crust on top was like stepping through shards of glass. My legs were raw and scraped through my fleece riding pants. No wonder my horse was so sluggish.

5) No-Wheelbarrow Snow.

This is the snow that is too deep, too icy, or too heavy to get the wheelbarrow from the stall to the manure pile. This calls for unusual barn management techniques, like the following:

- Continuously adding new bedding to the stalls to cover up the dirty part. You can shovel the layers out in the spring.
- Using a big tub on top of a saucer sled for the manure. This takes lots of trips. Tipping over the tub causes lots of swearing. (Note to self: write down phrases for next article: 100 Curses for Winter Horse People).
- Parking the wheelbarrow outside the stall door. Fill it with dirty bedding. Continue filling until wheelbarrow can no longer be seen. Then buy a new wheelbarrow. Repeat until spring.
- Throwing dirty bedding out of the stall into your horse's paddock. This works if the snow isn't too deep, and you aren't obsessive about clean paddocks. Note that the snow underneath the spread-out pile of dirty shavings won't thaw until about August. Think of it as a future swamp cooler for the horse's stall.
- Giving yourself a break if you are obsessive about clean paddocks (personally, I have good intentions and poor follow-through). Clean the paddock at the first thaw. The horse won't care- each snowfall gives him a clean surface anyhow.
- Shoveling a path through the deep snow just wide enough and long enough to get the wheelbarrow to the manure pile. Then, since at that point you will be too sore and tired to clean stalls, retreat to the house for a cup of hot cocoa, or something stronger.

6) Hoof-Packing snow.

This snow can be deceptive. At first it looks like Riding Snow. Once you get your horse saddled and head down the road, however, you notice that your 14-2 hand horse has grown a hand higher and is still growing. You look down, and he has built up four-inch platforms under his hooves. Do him a favor- get off, lead him home, and give him a treat. His legs and joints are worth preserving. Reward yourself with a cup of hot cocoa. Or Irish coffee.

7) Hot Cocoa Snow.

This is the kind of snow where you bundle up, saddle up, mount up, and it starts snowing wet wind-driven snow. My gelding hates walking into a frigid wet wind and tucks his head down lower and lower until it is practically curled under his belly. Just go home. No sense in having two miserable wet souls. Stall him, feed with hay, and have some more "cocoa."

If you are one of the brave souls who will ride in the winter, dress warm, beware of ice, and note that a good snowy day can turn a calm horse into a devious jokester. My mare's latest trick is starting to go down for a roll in the clean white stuff with no concern about me, or more importantly, the cost of my best saddle. Maybe it's a comment on my stall cleaning skills?

Forty-Five Dollars' Worth

I asked for a sled for my birthday. Not one of the wimpy, little-kid-hill sleds, more of a working sled. The kind you get at the big outdoor stores, a heavy-duty oversized tub of a sled, with an uplifted "bow" on the front like a small boat. I figured I could use the sled in the winter out in the horse barn for those times when the wheelbarrow becomes impossible to push in the snow and the stalls need cleaning.

The first snowy day in November we went to one of the outdoor stores in town, for snow boots and a few other things. We couldn't afford the over-priced snow boots for my teenager Mac and his still growing feet, however my pre-teen Chris and my husband Doug found the sled. It was black heavy-duty plastic. These sleds are made for hauling your gear out for ice fishing, or to pull behind a snowmobile. We needed it, and even though my birthday was still a month away, Doug and Chris got in line and paid 45 dollars for this useful barn tool. We could afford that; it was less than half the price of the snow boots we were considering.

We got home, and of course we had to try out the new sled. I'm not talking stall cleaning or working, that can always wait for another day, or another week. But my new horse was a Norwegian Fjord Horse. That little draft pony was made for snow and for pulling a sled. Now whether or not he had ever done this in his life was up for discussion. Whether I could actually steer him one-handed while holding the sled rope dallied (wrapped) around the saddle horn was another question. Oly was so much better to ride than he was when I first got him, but I had not trained him to neck-rein (one-handed steering). We had dragged several items on a rope behind us before, though never a glorified large plastic tub that made hissing sounds like a snake as we pulled it along the snow. Did I mention I hadn't ridden him in three weeks, and he might have some pent-up energy?

It was the wet kind of snow: 33 degrees and snowing. I told Mac and Chris to get dressed in their winter gear while I saddled Oly. I put his saddle on and walked him out to the small pasture. I pulled the sled along beside him while I was leading him from the ground. After one sideways glance at the giant hissing monster, he was over it, and walked calmly beside the sled. It was as though he'd been pulling sleds through snow for generations. I love this breed.

I discussed rules with my kids. I had to be able to let go of the sled from my end, and they needed to be able to let go from their end. You never know what a horse is going to do, and I wanted Oly to be able to get away from the scary rope or sled, and the kids to get away from potentially dangerous horse hooves. I loaded Chris in the sled, mounted, took up slack on the rope, made two twists around the saddle horn, and cued Oly to walk on. He started pulling, heard the sled coming behind him, and took off like a maniac. I dropped the pull-rope after Chris was pulled out of the sled, laughing, and quickly reined Oly to a stop. (Did you notice that part? Oly stopped after he shied. That was a huge improvement for this horse.) I then heard my trainer's words ringing in my head like sleighbells, "Train it from the ground before you try it in the saddle." Okay, a little late.

For the next try I led Oly, while also holding tension on the rope dally from his side. I thought one-handed steering would be hard. Now I was walking, leading, voice cuing, rope handling, and yelling directions at the kids all at the same time. It worked. Kids were sledding, the horse was pulling, and all was good until the next switch-out of kids, when Oly suddenly shied sideways around me until he was facing the sled. Snowballs. I hadn't said, "No throwing of snowballs!" and I had two siblings together outside in the snow. My Norwegian horse was not scared of sleds, he was scared of snowballs. Good instinct. I don't like snowballs either.

After we instituted the no-snowball rule, things went well. We discovered the tub-shaped sled didn't steer very well, unless the kids leaned so hard to the side that they fall out. Not a bad thing on the first snow day of the year. We also figured out that the rope from the saddle direct to the kids' hands, especially in sticky wet snow, made the steering even worse. The boys experimented with different ways to sit, and hold the rope, and try to steer. Maybe I'll break my rule and tie off on the sled side. I also learned that two kids on the sled in sticky snow was a bit heavy—the front part of the saddle actually lifted up off Oly's shoulders during the pulling. That's got to put some painful pressure on his back where the rear of the saddle pushes down. No complaints from my tough little guy, though. Note to self: add a "pulling breast collar" to birthday list. Or maybe an actual harness.

After we got everything put away, I was walking into the house with Chris. We were both soaking wet from the snow that was turning to rain. We were too happy to be cold.

"Chris, do you think that was 45 dollars' worth of fun?"

"Yep. That was definitely 45 dollars' worth of fun."

We both can't wait for the next snow. I was thinking about putting a saddle horn on the sled side, so they can dally the rope on the sled, too. Wouldn't that be cool, a sled with a saddle horn? I have an old broken pony saddle decorating my porch. I wonder how that horn is affixed? I'll have to put my engineer boys on the problem.

Sledding with Oly. Photo credit Margaret Eames.

Water in Winter

Horses drink a lot. Up to 20 gallons a day. Even on the coldest winter days they need plenty of clean, unfrozen water. Keeping a full trough thawed is a challenge. Spokane can have mellow winters and hard winters. The mellow winters are full of rain and mud. The hard winters can be 27 degrees below zero. That is cold enough to freeze a large horse trough solid in a day or two. Some winters are in between, though feel never-ending.

The nicest barns, with the smartest owners, have heated, individual, on-demand waterers in each stall. I've never seriously investigated those, mainly because I'm cheap. But also because they would require buried waterlines and electric lines. Our soil is about four inches deep and less in most places, with solid basalt rock below. Most of my fence lines are crooked because it's so hard to get a post in the ground through the rock. Running a buried pipe or cable deep enough to avoid freezing is next to impossible.

Since moving to Spokane a couple decades ago, I've tried various methods to keep troughs thawed in the winter. Our first winter here, with one horse, I tried the ax method. When the trough freezes over you use an ax to break a drinking hole in the middle of the trough. Actually, the first frozen night when the ice is thin you can use the heel of your boot, although be careful, since it's easy to misjudge the strength needed, and you can end up with a boot full of ice water. I know this. Eventually though, if the cold snap continues, you need an ax or similar tool to get through the ice. You not only need to break the ice, you also must pull the giant hunk of ice out with your hands. Bare hands. When it's 10 degrees out. In order to keep the opening thawed for a while, you also need to bring a bucket full of hot water to add to the trough. At my house, the hot water needs to come from the kitchen, since there is no heated water outside. Imagine carrying full buckets of warm water out to the horse, in your heavy winter boots, down the hall, out the porch, down the steps, and across the snowy, icy lawn to the barn. It never sloshes over the bucket, onto your pants, and into your boots. Ever. Nor do your pants freeze after that happens. Nor are you ever late for work due to the need to change clothes.

Eventually after a couple of years, intelligent person that I am, I learned about trough heaters. These electric heaters come in varying designs, but they all include a submersible heating coil. Some are for plastic troughs; some are for metal troughs. Some can be attached to a wire basket to keep the heater from touching the edge of a plastic trough and melting a hole through the edge, which would totally defeat the purpose of a trough heater. All require an extension cord run out to wherever the horse trough is. This is despite the fact that the labels say to plug the heater directly into an outlet and avoid use of extension cords. As noted before, running an underground line out to where I need it doesn't really work at our house, so we use the extension cord method despite the well-meaning advice from the manufacturers. They obviously have no idea what real horse owners are facing.

We currently have two troughs for two horses, and we snake the long cords over the barn rafters, and along the top of stalls to connect to the short trough-heater cord. Once they're plugged together tight, we wrap the connection with black tape, and if the connection's exposed to the weather, we do an additional wrap with a plastic bag and more tape.

I have learned two lessons about trough heaters. Lesson 1: As much as possible, keep the cord out of reach of the horses. Some horses are playful and view the heater on a cord as a tremendously entertaining toss-toy. I've never had a horse electrocuted yet; however, I've had them pull the heater out and sculpt its wire frame into new and unusual shapes. My horse Oly will play with the heater if the water level gets too low. He uses it as a drum stick on the side of the trough to bring me out of the house to investigate the weird sounds, and then to fill up the troughs. Which brings us to Lesson 2: Don't let the water level get below the heater coil. It doesn't work if there is no water around it.

To keep the troughs full at our house, we run a hose from the standpipe on one side of the barn, stretched around to the trough on the other side of the barn. When it's 10 degrees out, hoses freeze, especially when you have forgotten to drain them the last time you filled the troughs, because the week before the weather was unseasonably warm. A few days later, during the arctic blast, you notice that the hose is still loosely looped on the ground, and so full of ice it doesn't want to bend. You unhook the iced-up hose and lay it flat along the fence to wait for the next thaw, hopefully out of the way of the snowblower path, just in case there's a real snowfall. We have a lot of hoses hanging along our fence, in lovely drapes along the wood poles, much like Christmas swags along stair rail posts in a house that is clean, neatly painted, and well-decorated because the owner doesn't have outdoor animals sucking up all her time, what with thawing hoses and filling horse troughs and all.

After realizing that the draped hoses do not really count as Christmas decorations, even though they are green (and maybe I could add a string of lights), I focus on the task at hand and pull off a shorter hose, one that won't reach around the barn, but will reach if I take a short-cut through a stall to the second horse trough. I fasten on the new hose, lift the spigot handle, and nothing happens. This hose is also frozen. I can tell, because instead of the water going out the hose end, the pressure is forcing it up through the top connector, out the side of the faucet, and all over my left pant leg. Did I mention it's 10 degrees out?

There is a trick to thawing hoses that works if the troughs are not too low, and if you have a trough heater. You coil the frozen hose down into the heated water of the trough. That works for me because one of my troughs actually is right next to the standpipe so I can leave it hooked up while thawing. I know that sounds surprisingly efficient and forward-thinking of me, but it's true, the first trough is right there. It can take a while but eventually the ice in the coiled hose loosens and the water pressure shoots it out and it floats to the top in little one inch ice cylinders, adding a bit of festivity to my horse's winter drink. But now that the frozen hose is thawed, I need to pull it out, yard by yard, getting my gloves completely soaked in the process. But at least the first trough is now full. For the second trough at our house, I have to go through a stall, which I have just cleaned and placed dry shavings in. So I kink the end of the hose, doubling it back on itself so the stall doesn't get wet and in the process I get my other pant leg soaked. But the stall stays dry so it's all good.

Finally, with my wet, gloved fingers and pant legs beginning to freeze solid, both water troughs are filled. I turn off the hose, pull it back through the stall, and lay it end down into a low spot in the yard. I unhook it from the faucet, and lift one end over my head, draining it as I hold it high and walk, lifting, frozen hand by frozen hand until all water drains out the low end. I hang it with the other decorative hose swags over the fence posts, to wait another three days to do it all over again, whereupon I find out, that despite my careful draining, the hose still has frozen parts. Back to the thawing in the horse trough method. This usually continues all winter, with the only variables being how long it takes, and how much of my clothes are wet and frozen before I'm done. One winter was further complicated because the water pipe broke near the barn, so we had to run water from the outdoor spigots by the house, requiring even more length of frozen hose. But guess what we found? A HEATED HOSE! It requires an outlet, and we don't keep it plugged in when not in use. It has been a huge help to keep that water flowing. Come on, spring!

Buying Breeches

I was looking at my winter polar fleece riding pants and noticed the scissor slices through the elastic waistband. I wore these when I was pregnant with Mac and needed more give at the waist. That made them about 17 years old. Somehow, they had become generally snug all around, more like tights than pants. Even though I still look lean and tall from a distance, up close I'm getting middle-aged pooches here and there. I really don't want to emphasize all my curves these days. Those pants weren't really riding pants anyway, they're more like polar fleece outerwear that one would wear cross-country skiing. I don't ski cross-country now; I bruise too easy with the constant falling down. But I do still ride, and those pants have a slick finish on the outside. Good riding pants, or breeches, have at least a sticky suede-like patch at the knee. That's not there for looks, it's there to help you stay in the saddle when your horse decides to go a different direction than you're expecting. At speed. My current horse does that a lot. He sometimes decides that heels up and buck is the right answer when I am saying go forward. Sticky knee pads are better than slick nylon when we are having our directional disagreements. Therefore, I needed a new pair of winter riding pants.

I'm really rather cheap. It's my Scottish side. I'm the one who lectures the family on frugalness and saving money. My family generally ignores me. But after all those lectures, can I just head out to the tack store right before Christmas and buy myself some winter breeches? We're talking $125 and up, for a pair of pants. But yes, I can do this, because I have a 25 percent-off coupon for one item at the local tack store. I am practically saving money just walking in the door with my coupon that expires December 31. Plus, are talking warm, soft, fuzzy-inside pants, and we may yet get winter weather sometime this year. The winter breeches are calling me. So are those winter riding boots over in the corner of the tack store. But first, the pants.

I grab a medium pair and a large pair. The medium pair should fit me, based on the label, but the large pair is longer for my long legs. I try the medium pair on. They're snug and fit like tights. Super tight tights. Who knew I had such an obvious panty line and even an obvious sock line? My horse isn't going to care if I show off my butt. Between the two of us, my horse's butt is way cuter and he gets all the looks anyhow. I peel off and wriggle out of the medium pair and try the large pair. Aaaah . . . sort of a cross between a warm blanket, comfy yoga pants, and sweats. Not the most flattering pair of breeches ever, what with a little extra cloth that might wrinkle at the thigh, and the barely tight enough waist that might require a belt if I ever wear them to an actual horse event, but there are belt loops for that eventuality. I can even see myself wearing these around the house on a cold winter day.

I hand the large pair and the coupon to the clerk and try on some insulated riding boots. Luckily for me, they are out of my size, and I escape the store with only a pair of breeches, and some cool, plastic emergency-release tie-up clips for the horse trailer that I didn't know I needed until I saw them.

On Christmas morning I pulled my unwrapped breeches out from under the tree, and wore them for the next two days solid, despite our moderate above-freezing weather. But I hear it's supposed to snow soon, and I have the comfiest, outdoor-yoga-stall-cleaning-snowshoeing-snow-shoveling-riding pants ever. Come on, snow! One of these days, I might even wear them on a horse.

I'm still considering some new winter boots. If only I can finagle a 25 percent-off coupon somewhere.

Winter Doldrums

he winter darkness and cold weather usually starts bothering me in January, some years more than others. Is it my age? Is it the long, wet fall (okay . . . it's all a blur—was it a long wet fall? Or was that last year?). The winter after both my horses came up lame was the worst. I felt cheated out of riding time. On those glum dark days, I started looking for reasons to be with the horses. What can one do with short day length and snow on the ground? I figured I'm not the first person to ask this question, so of course I Googled it. You can find small-space training articles online. I need to look at those more closely, and start implementing them.

I've been finding my own things to do with my horses. I don't work them too hard or too long, especially when they are recuperating from injuries. Here is my version of things to do with horses in the winter. Of course, if you have an indoor arena, it's all different, and I don't want to talk to you. Unless it's good horse-hauling weather, then you might be my new best friend.

Clean the tack room.

Although I would always rather work with horses than clean, the barn slightly outranks the house when it comes to cleaning chores. Cleaning the barn and tack room on the real cruddy days gets me outside. Lately, we have had challenges with mouse turds. We had a population explosion of mice a couple years ago and they are still hanging around. Our barn cat is fat and happy, and I'm not sure if he even catches mice, or whether he just bats them around a little. But the tack room can get pretty gross. Even when it's below freezing, I still spray some cleaner or bleach on the mouse piles before sweeping them up. I haven't caught hantavirus yet so it must be working. Anyhow, cleaning up, hanging up, and boxing up in a tack room can take a whole winter afternoon, and you feel so productive afterwards! You also feel cold.

Practice tying, or highlining.

There are some days when the footing sucks: either it's too muddy, or the snow is building up in the horses' hooves, or it's just plain old slippery. But standing tied is always a good idea. Working with one horse, while the other is tied is good for their sensitive, little horse psyches. Okay, it's only my young one that has a sensitive green-horse psyche. Still, standing tied is good for all ages to practice.

Drag things.

We drag things like a bag of cans or a cargo sled. In the winter we drag from the ground, getting the young horse used to strange things. It can be entertaining. One day Vali stepped inside the sled, and another time he bit the edge with his mouth and lifted it. You don't really get to understand your horse's sense of humor until you spend some down time and some ground time with them.

Practice groundwork in the round pen.

When the footing is good, we do some classic groundwork, turning, changing gaits, or moving backward or forward to a lead-rope wiggle. It's mostly walk and trot until the footing gets better, but it improves the horse's respect level.

Take walks.

When my horses were recuperating, we did a lot of walking and trotting in hand. I loved the 40-minute walks with the horse. Sometimes in sucky weather, it can be more like a 15-minute slog through heavy footing. But the horses like getting out of their paddocks and walking the property boundaries.

Try massage or acupressure.

I bought a book on equine acupressure and have been experimenting on the horses. I'm not sure it's healing or helping anything, however some of the reactions to the pressure points are interesting. A lot of horses like massage. An electric massager can offer some bonding time on a rainy day.

Play with toys.

I try to give the horses toys to stay occupied. I'm not sure they make a difference. I had a sock monkey tied up in a stall for a while; it's now a dirt-colored blob in the paddock. My horses have had times when they eat fence boards for entertainment. When it's above freezing, I can have the delightful

105

job of painting a deterrent on the boards. The equivalent of horse toys for me includes books. Horse books, riding books, training books, shopping catalogs . . . After all that reading, I'll be better prepared for the spring horse challenges once the weather finally turns.

Clean tack.

We've already established that cleaning isn't my thing. Nonetheless, a couple times a year I give my gear a deep clean and follow it up with oiling. Both help the gear last, and given the cost, it better last. In the winter I usually bring the gear into the house for this task.

Create.

Learn to braid baling twine. Invent new tack out of baling twine. Crochet a saddle blanket. (Really, my aunt did once!) Or crochet a fly bonnet for your horse's ears.

Exercise.

Get in shape for the riding season by shoveling up the poop-sicles and manure icebergs. Use a pickaxe to break the ice. Do weight training with full buckets of water: faucet to pens, faucet to pens. Repeat. Count the calories you are burning! Follow up with hot cocoa.

Plan stuff.

Plan your year of horse riding, researching locations and fun trips. Or do what I do and wait for a friend to plan a whole summer of rides and join her when you can.

Buy stuff.

Shop for riding jeans, and cool horse doodads online. Invest in a good set of Yaktrax or other traction devices for your boots, so you can get from the house to the barn when your yard is a sheet of ice.

Groom your horse.

Trim his mane. This is most fun on a Fjord Horse's two-color mane. Practice braiding manes and tails. Put silly hats on your horse and take a selfie. Share it on social media.

Dream.

Price out the cost to build an indoor arena. Gasp. Go outside and shovel more manure to get over the sticker shock. Decide your front pasture makes a fine place to ride after all.

Exercise some more.

Take up skijoring! Or take up ice skating in your round pen. Put on your snowshoes and visit potential riding trails. This is SO much harder than riding.

Leave town.

Take your horse to Arizona and do some horse camping. Or go to a horse expo in a warmer location. Horse expos sell tack, and we all need a little something new to brighten up our winter.

The Case of the Fjord in the Springtime, or Vali Meets His Match

Imagine if you will, a sumo wrestler with a rope around his chin and forehead. Imagine little old you, using that rope, tugging to ask him to turn left, and that sumo wrestler saying, "No thank you! I'm going this way back to my buddy, and too bad if you are in my way. I will also nonchalantly kick out at you as I rush by!" Can you stop this surprisingly fast sumo wrestler from going where he wants with that little rope around his head? No. By sumo wrestler, I mean Fjord Horse. This is what it was like my second spring with Vali the Younger. Fjords are short, solid (some would say fat), and opinionated. After the second incident of Vali pulling the lead rope out of my hand, and running past while kicking out toward me, I knew I had trouble.

How do I get myself into these things? I see a horse that's cute, has decent conformation, is sort of rideable and still green, and doesn't buck (they said). I'm a moderately good rider. I've had green horses before and did great with them. Getting this horse going should be easy, I thought. But one year later, after a winter off, I had my hands full. Or rather, I had my hands empty each time he pulled away to go where he wanted. I needed someone more skilled than me to work this horse. Even if I decided not to keep him, he needed training before I could sell him. So, I put the word out.

I considered a trainer in Moses Lake, an hour and a half away, and a trainer in Post Falls, Idaho, 45 minutes away. I had a line on another trainer down by Lewiston, Idaho. Then I got a call from a friend of a friend. She rides event horses, among other disciplines, and trains project horses on the side. She needed another project for the spring. She has ridden forever and trained many horses. Plus, her barn was relatively close to home, so I could watch and learn as she worked my spoiled pony.

I remember the April day I brought Vali to Jean's house. I was worried about getting him from the trailer to her fenced area without trouble. We got him contained inside the fence on her property, and Jean took over. My leading style was too timid. I had lost my confidence with Vali, and he knew it. That is one difference between trainers, and riders. Every movement of that horse is a training opportunity. With a trainer, the first step off the trailer is a time to be focused on the dominant human. No lapses of concentration are allowed. Immediately Jean was enforcing her space and expecting obedience. I left Vali with Jean for a month, and asked Jean to give me honest feedback at the end of the month on his suitability as a trail horse and on my suitability as his owner.

Jean started working him on day one and worked him every single day of that month. Initially we had texts and emails back and forth about what he knew and what he didn't know. The list of things he knew was short. Even with Jean, Vali started out pushy and disobedient. She spent most of her training time on groundwork and lunging in circles with the cotton line connected through the bit rings and under the jaw. With most horses, running the line through the bit is a strong way to make corrections of behavior. Nonetheless, I remember vividly Jean's text message describing a very bad day. She sent me pictures of the bruises on her thigh from when she was lunging Vali, and he got that look in his eye and bolted, causing the lunge line to get tangled around Jean's leg. She was drug across the arena, basically by the strength of Vali's jaw. Jean said she was sure she was a goner, but he stopped, she untangled herself, and then gave herself a lecture about getting caught up in the line. After that day she upped the arsenal of control mechanisms. She added a chain to the end of the lead rope and lunge line. The chain through the bit rings, or over the nose, is an old-fashioned technique in this era of rope halters and gentle persuasion, however this was an old-fashioned, bull-necked horse. Jean needed a strength equalizer.

After seeing the giant bruises that resulted from the lunging incident, running from her hip down the extent of her thigh, I offered to find another trainer. "Nah," she said, "We'll get through this. The tangling up was my own fault." I worried for her, but we kept on.

Not long after that, Jean reported on the second very bad day with Vali. It wasn't bad for her, just for him. The chain method was well established, and he had learned he couldn't get away. However, he hadn't fully submitted to the iron will of his trainer. She was lunging him, and he came to a corner in the arena, and tried to spin away from Jean to avoid her command. He turned outside toward the arena fence, forcing the lunge line tight along his body, and Jean just braced her weight onto the line. Vali stopped, head by the fence, body facing the wrong direction, the line back around his haunch, and with nowhere to move. Jean basically sat back on the line and waited. And waited. Vali leaned against the pressure, facing the wrong way, and leaned . . . and leaned . . . unable to move forward. He leaned, chain and bit pressure tight on his jaw. She waited and watched. Minutes went by. Jean never lessened the pressure. Finally, Vali chewed, sighed, and turned back around to release the pressure. Jean praised him, let him think for a few minutes on a loose line, and put him right back to work. That was the day everything changed. It's not that he didn't test her again, but after that he would give in promptly.

Fjords are solid like a sumo wrestler and opinionated like a Norwegian. They are also smart. Vali learned that he could not win an argument with Jean, at least not in the long term. So he settled down to work. By the end of the month, he was walking, trotting, and cantering on the lunge and under saddle obediently. We did some test trail rides, first with me on Oly, and Jean on Vali, then with me on Vali. He was quite good on trails. Jean sent him back to me, confident that he would do better and better with experience. On the condition that I continue to use the chain during groundwork for at least a year.

Jean was right. I rode him as much as I could that spring and summer on the trail and in lessons. He continued to improve and became a very solid trail horse. Vali still tested me a few times, but with the techniques Jean taught me, and the strength equalizer, I was able to win those battles of will.

I am indebted to Jean for her help in finding the good horse under the spoiled horse. He truly changed with consistent work and understanding of the rules. His eye changed, from almost constantly anxious, to soft, and he got more mellow and embraced his inner lazy Fjord Horse personality. I looked forward to many long trail rides on my reclaimed horse.

I am also indebted to Jean for giving me some great horsewoman quotes during our training time together, such as:

"I was ready to shoot him. That's why I don't carry."

"I might have him trained before my bruises heal."

"I told my husband that if he is ever investigated for domestic violence, to bring my horse friends in as witnesses to explain the bruising."

A Ribbon by Any Other Name Is a Rose

As the proud owner of a green horse, I began putting a green ribbon in my horse's tail. Green meaning, well, *green*, in the horse world. Or, *My horse is young and unpredictable, don't crowd me!* I found that the green ribbon was not respected or recognized by others, and after my horse kicked another, we changed to red. Red means *I kick! Back off!* I found that there is some debate about the meaning of ribbons; it depends on where you are from. Nevertheless, the ones I know for sure are red for kickers if tied in the tail, red for biters if tied on the forelock, and green for green horse. Personally, I'm sticking with red, until my horse becomes more predictable. Although, when I can't find my red ribbon, I've been known to braid a red plastic rose into his tail.

Vali with Red Ribbon. Photo credit Cindy Miller.

It's a Numbers Game,
or CRS—Can't Remember Squat Disease

Sometimes I have a riding lesson where everything is going right, the horse is soft and graceful, and we ride in partnership like ballet dancers. All is right with the world. My teacher guides us to improve step by step, verbally adjusting my body or my rein, until I feel like I am riding a new and perfectly obedient horse. Then a few days later I'm back in the saddle at home trying to reproduce that lovely ride. It's like riding a giraffe in a field of giant boulders. How did we get to that balanced and listening place together? Yeah, we can move forward, yet there is no grace, no flow, no controlled power. What did we do on that last ride with help, and why can't I remember the steps to get there now?

Three. Three is all I can keep in my brain. I now have the rule of three. If I'm stopping at the grocery store, I can remember three items, however if there are more than three, I must write them down. This holds true with riding lessons, too. After 45 minutes of riding with my teacher and following her instructions, my horse and I finally work together to move in precision and balance. By the end of the lesson, we are tired and happy and riding better than the last lesson. I ask myself, how did we get that big trot again? It seems like we did 42 different adjustments to get there.

But then I come back to my rule of three. At the end of the lesson, I ask my instructor, what three things did we work on today, and of all the things, which three do I need to practice? My teacher understands me, and she lists out the three key things. She knows, and I know, that if I don't digest my lesson down to a limited number of tasks that by the time I walk my horse the 100 yards to my truck to write it down, it will be gone. In that five-minute walk it will fly away with the flock of a thousand other things I am trying and failing to remember. It is pushing my limited mental capacity to even remember those three things long enough to get to my truck. With focus, I can do it.

I looked up the psychology of remembering items, and the average human can hold five to seven objects in their short-term memory. I do remember my first phone number in my hometown. Initially our local numbers were five digits, and eventually they became seven digits. Though to be precise, these numbers are enmeshed in my long-term memory now, not short-term. Obviously though, I am below average in my short-term memory capability since I have my own rule of only three items.

Just writing down the three lesson tasks once I'm back at the truck helps me with remembering. I have little bits of paper spread all over my truck and house with lesson summaries, and they don't often make it out to the barn with me for the next ride. Since I wrote it down, though, I can usually remember what I need to be working on.

Breaking big riding ideas into a limited number of tasks for my brain is similar to how we are taught to train horses, too. You don't get on a green horse and ask him to immediately turn perfect serpentine lines around a row of cones. You train small steps at a time. Here, give to the pressure of this rein first by turning your head. Great, now that you know that, follow the pressure and follow your nose into a turn at a walk. A turn at a time, a step at a time, step by step, one two three. Simplifying lessons into small additive steps for the horse, and small memory steps for the human, gets us to the same place. Four years into my journey with Vali, we are still working on the perfect serpentine through a line of cones. On our riding journey, we're making progress.

Speaking of counting to three and higher, this will be my year to count. There are many social media horse groups that track things: 100 rides, 100 miles, 500 miles. This year I will join the counts, and track my progress on numbers of rides, miles of rides, and locations of rides. When the weather improves, I may try 30 rides in 30 days. A trainer friend swears by 30 days straight for green horses. While Vali is no longer green, I think 30 days of focus will still be good for us. Maybe 21 straight days of rides for early 2021. Or 22 days of rides for early 2022.

I also have trouble remembering gear. I have lists of things to pack. Every time before heading off to a trail ride or a lesson, I check my mental list. This list is not a list of three, it's more a mental list of the final steps of tacking up the horse and checking that I have everything I'll need to ride.

1. Saddle and girth.
2. Bridle.

3. Saddle pad.
4. Helmet.
5. Whip.

Most other things I can do without, but those I need to ride. Once I forgot my riding boots. I don't have boots on my final mental list, because they are usually on my feet. I rode that day in my slip-on clogs. Riding boots are a safety thing, the heel keeps your foot from getting stuck in the stirrup. I figured my foot would slide easily out of my clogs in a pinch, so I didn't feel un-safe. I could always ride without stirrups if I had to.

Of course, I can ride without a whip, but my horse knows if I don't have it. For us, a whip is another aid. It is an extension of my arm, or an emphasis to my leg. It is not to beat my horse. The whip is to tell him, yes, I'm serious about that squeeze of legs that means go. Because I ride an opinionated draft pony, he is not always sensitive to aids. He is quite sure that every new or changed aid means to slow down, or to stop. He tests me regularly. In one of our lessons, when we were finally cantering well and I was saying with my body, keep going, keep going, keep going, he got tired and did a sudden emphatic four-legged total halt. He was testing whether that was now the answer to the "go" aids, testing whether I was serious. I rode that cow-horse halt, and immediately pushed him back into the canter with the help of the whip, laughing out loud. He's like a Shetland pony constantly testing its kid.

Anyhow, whips. I have four dressage whips (medium length), and a shorter crop. I can locate two of my dressage whips right now. I have no doubt the other ones will show up again. They always do. I have a cheap plastic black whip that I marked with stripes of white and fluorescent orange duct tape. The black, white, and orange stripes are reminiscent of a coral snake. This is my road riding whip. If I am on the shoulder of the road, I hold it straight out sideways, and it's visible to cars to give me room on my unpredictable steed. It helps; however they still come too close. I lost that special whip for months. I was sure I had left it on my trailer fender after a ride, and it was laying in the ditch along some road somewhere. Then my husband found it in the tool shed. It was apparently visiting with the snowblower. Yay!

While the "caution-snake" whip was missing, I bought another nice dressage whip at my favorite tack store. It was German, not cheap. It was the right length and weight, and it balanced nicely in the hand. I brought it home, showed it off to my family, and never saw it again. I was starting to wonder if I had really gotten it home from the store. Finally, one day my mom was vacuuming the stairs, and found my whip tucked in at the bottom crease of the first stair step. It was the perfect size and color to disappear, camouflaged, like a snake in a shadow. I was happy to be reunited with my new whip, knowing it was only a matter of time before I lost it, or one of the others again.

Sometimes, despite my best intentions, I do forget my whip when I go on a trail ride. My mental checklist fails, and the whip never makes it to the trailer. Vali knows when I don't have a whip, because he is basically a giant pony with a pony brain. But my riding buddies usually have an extra whip stashed away. When I borrow one, I try oh-so-hard to get it back to their trailer tack room, so that it's there the next time I need to borrow it. One time, Karen's trailer door was locked and I placed her borrowed whip on the trailer fender while I unsaddled. I was sure I would remember to put it inside the tack area once the door was unlocked. Karen texted me later that day to let me know that her whip had ridden on the fender all the way home. I was so lucky. That would have required another whip purchase at the tack store to replace it.

Then there are gloves. I like to ride with gloves, since my horse is stronger than me and has been known to pull reins and lead ropes out of my hands. There's nothing like dealing with a rope burn in addition to the frustration of chasing a loose horse across the yard toward his buddy. I wear gloves for grip and protection. Also, I lose gloves. Regularly. I probably have five pairs of true riding gloves, and a couple more pairs of medium-weight, general-use gloves. I think I could find three pairs at this moment. They often get lost in pairs, but sometimes as individuals. Sometimes they come back from the void and visit with me for a while; sometimes they stay away for a year, or 10. I blame the gloves for these mysterious travels. Surely it is not me who misplaces them. I do believe that my coats are sometimes in cahoots with my gloves, though. Perhaps the coat pockets provide the portal for glove travel. One second, they're there, and the next second, they're not, only to reappear the next winter, innocently visiting that coat pocket again. I wish the coats would stop colluding with the gloves. I wish all my gear would stay in its assigned place. But for that, I would have to remember to put it away. And we know how bad my memory is.

Mud Season

After the winter of the never-ending snow and ice, I knew it had to come. Mud season. Even though I dreaded mud, I began to look at it with a certain sense of glee. Mud means the snow's gone and riding season is here!

My house is west of Spokane, Washington, in an area with shallow soil over basalt rock. It takes a long time for water to drain. Between packed snow and ice, and then the pineapple-express rainstorms we got one year, we ended up with an overabundance of water. The water bodies at my house were big enough we named them: Pasture Pond, Yard Pond, Breezeway Bay, Horse Trailer Lake, Gramma's Creek, Goat Barn Pond, and many more. Our garage flooded and we couldn't get from the carport to the house without rubber boots. We were thinking of getting the canoe out to visit the neighbors.

My horse paddocks were morasses of manure and mud. I couldn't get the wheelbarrow through the muck to clean out a winter's worth of manure. All I could do was make temporary piles in the paddocks and wait for them to dry. In normal years we get a seasonal pond in the back pasture; this year it was gigantic and encroached on the paddocks. The boys in my family, including my husband, all become hydrological engineers. They used hoes and shovels to connect puddles to other puddles, weaving little streams through the paddocks back to the giant pond. They gleefully re-sculpted the ditches until water was flowing downstream away from the stalls, so there was at least one dry spot for the horses to stand in.

Eventually I built temporary fencing for the horses in the only high spot on the property under the pines. I wasn't sure my new young horse would respect the electric fence, but he did. The Fjord Horses didn't really mind the mud. I think it bothered me more than them. However, they loved having a little grass to nibble in their new pasture. Horses look forward to spring with as much glee as humans.

That spring all the seasonal ponds in the neighborhood edged up to the roads, and several areas of our gravel road deteriorated. The gravel was losing the battle with the mud and becoming mush. It was amazing to watch as the road finally thawed and changed due to super-saturation. First there were big potholes, then there was a bouncy trampoline effect to the road. It was like a layer of gravel and clay was perched over bubbles of water. It was the texture of bread dough, or jello. Then it became ridges of gravel with ruts, and little mud volcanoes appeared. Finally, the road changed to true, deep mud in areas. It had the consistency of chocolate pudding.

I was leery of hauling the horse trailer through the mud bogs and wasn't even sure I could get a loaded trailer out of Horse Trailer Lake without getting stuck. Even the round pen became a boggy mess. I was limited to working my horses on our quiet road between the mud holes. At least the road was soft on their hooves. That spring the horses got considerable practice with water crossings. If the roads got worse, I knew I could ride a horse out in an emergency. Plus, I knew that by August when it's 100 degrees out, I would miss the water and mud. In the meantime, though, I was dreading skeeter season.

Skeeter Season

Spring has sprung, summer is right behind it, the flowers are blooming, the grass needs mowing, and the mosquitoes are flying and biting with a vengeance! It's not like I've never been around mosquitoes before, after all I grew up on the wet side of the state, but it's pretty intense this year.

Some of the worst mosquitoes I remember were when I was a kid and went camping with my family at Lake Wenatchee State Park in Central Washington. The mosquitoes were so bad there that we spent most of the weekend zipped into the tent watching the kamikazes dive at the mesh, trying to get to us. Even our dog couldn't stand it outside.

As a college student I was lucky enough to work on a research project down the road from Lake Wenatchee, based out of a cabin at Fish Lake. I believe it's called Fish Lake because if the locals had given it a more honest name like, say, Mosquito Hordes Lake, no one would visit. We would do our surveys out in the woods and have contests to see how many mosquitoes we could kill with a one-hand-slap on our thigh. My record was 14. For mosquito repellent, we had super-strength DEET. No one knows what DEET stands for, but it does work. It also takes the paint off a pencil. I was not convinced it was safe to use on bare skin, nonetheless there were times I used it.

This year Spokane is competing with those notorious mosquito havens of Western and Central Washington. We always get some mosquitoes in the spring in the West Plains. This wet year, however, I am not convinced they'll ever leave. In mid-May I noticed the mosquitoes were getting smaller. I thought maybe it was the beginning of the end and they were getting stressed and running out of puddles to breed in. Then it rained. For three days. In mid-June I thought we were nearing the end again; I would only get three mosquitoes attacking my arm when I brought the horses in from pasture in the evening. And guess what? It rained. We still have plenty of mosquito habitat left.

Meanwhile, the horses are being eaten alive. They have hundreds of itchy welts on the areas of thinner hair on their necks and faces. I'm on a quest to find a repellent that works. Some years I use hardly any bug repellents on the horses. This year I was already on my third bottle of skeet-juice by the third week of May. I'm talking about the good stuff, with the long chemical names that fill up the whole label that you have to squint at to read. It probably has DEET in it. Usually, I try the wimpy herbal stuff, that barely works, because I honestly think it's better for the horses. This year they deserve some relief until the weather dries up and the mosquitoes leave.

The thing is, I haven't found anything super effective, and certainly not super long lasting. The mega-chemicals seem to do best, and maybe slow the mosquitoes, but not stop them. The repellents that say they will last several days are lucky to last several hours. I've tried Avon's Skin-So-Soft, and it worked. For about half an hour. Years and years ago when I had a sensitive and itchy horse, I tried things like garlic powder in the grain, apple cider vinegar in the grain and topically, and B-vitamins. I never really noticed much difference, although it surely didn't hurt the horse. I continue to look for the magic recipe for a safe and healthy mosquito repellent that I can make at home AND that works. In the meantime, if you all know of any good skeet-juice recipes that work, or even if you've found a store-bought repellent that is super effective, be sure to share it. The horses will love you for it.

Spring Resolutions

Yes, I know, resolutions are traditionally for January, not April, but it feels like the year is new in spring. The snow is gone and the pasture is showing green—thus, spring resolutions! Spring always makes me think of where I want to go, and what I want to do with my horse. Spring also makes me think of my bucket list for rides and accomplishments. Maybe I should call it The Grain Bucket List. I have the Summer Grain Bucket List, and the Long-Term Grain Bucket List. I have learned that a big list with big tasks can seem overwhelming. If you break each big task into little sub-tasks, everything is reachable in time.

Here's a recent Summer Grain Bucket list for the riding year, with tasks and sub-tasks:

1. Turn my younger horse into a solid, predictable riding horse.
   Yeah, I know, this can take years. But I will make progress on him this summer.
   - Hire a trainer to put time on him.
   - Take him to the local de-spooking clinic.
   - Get him out on the trail in small groups with sane horses.
   - Ride, ride, ride. Practice, practice, practice.

2. Ride in new places on new trails.
   Luckily, I have a friend who loves to get out to new places. I can usually just go along and don't have to do much planning for this.

3. Sell an old saddle and buy a new saddle for the young horse.
   - Advertise or consign the old saddle.
   - Wait to buy a new saddle until old saddle is sold.
   - Lose money on old saddle and pay big bucks on new saddle.

4. Get all the truck and trailer repairs and maintenance done early, so I'm safe when heading out on the trail.

   Okay, I'm flunking this part so far. I used the truck and trailer yesterday, and the trailer brakes are grabbing.

   - Make an appointment with mechanic.
   - Remember appointment.
   - Pay big bucks.

5. Go riding with an old friend.

   My old horsey friends are from the west side of the State, and getting over there is a bit of a haul.

   - Call old friends, check on schedule, pick a place to ride, and a weekend.
   - Sign up together for a training clinic at a central location. That also nicely meshes with item one, getting the younger horse trained better.

6. Ride in a wilderness area (an item on my Long-Term Grain Bucket List).

   This might be next year, not this year. It might be on foot, or on horseback. It might be on my horse, or I might hire a packer. It might be Glacier Peak wilderness, or the Pasayten. Or maybe "The Bob" (the Bob Marshall Wilderness). I definitely need to work toward this long-term goal.

   - Research trails and locations.
   - Learn to pack.
   - Research horse packer businesses.

Here's to a joyful spring! May your horses be sound and your trails amazing.

Spring Horses

Riding horses on windy days is like riding a coiled spring. Any quick move by you or a blade of grass and the horses are off—hopping, bucking, grinning . . . the spring has sprung. Even when it's fun and you're grinning with them you need to remind them to shape up and knock it off. It's poor manners. If you don't reprimand them, they'll do it more and more often, and when you ask them to buckle down and get to work, they buck instead. Professionalism at all times, just like at the office. But way more fun . . .

Scene Through a Horseman's Eye

It's all about the eye. Horsemen and horsewomen talk about a "soft eye." A soft eye is a large horse eye that appears kind. A doe-eyed puppy kind of look. Some horses have it all the time. Like Oly the Elder. He has a large eye in proportion to his face, and he is a kind, affectionate horse. Many horsemen look for that characteristic in a new horse. Me, I have a foot fetish. I look for a large, strong hoof proportionate to the horse's body. But most of my horses have also had a kind eye.

Vali, not so much initially. He had a medium eye. It was not real small; that's a fault that old-timers say indicates pigheadedness. It's actually called a pig-eye. Vali's eye was also not really large, like Oly's. We'll call it a proportionate eye. But Vali has great feet!

Eventually I learned that Vali had a strong streak of Norwegian stubbornness. I can say that, because I'm part Norwegian, right? Anyhow, at a certain point in our relationship, I started to think Vali's eye had an evil, nervous glint. I did not see kindness; I saw an opinionated cleverness. I especially saw it during his pulling-out-of-my-hand escapades. But after his training, his eye changed. I didn't know a horse's eye would change. With his attitude change, and increased submissiveness and obedience, he just looked softer and more attentive.

We trail riders have an eye, too. It is an eye that is always looking at scenery as we drive by, and thinking, *could I ride there?* I'm sure it's the same way river rafters look at rivers, scuba divers look at shorelines, and mountain climbers look at rocky slopes. We trail riders look at the ridges, open land and forests, and think, *Is it too brushy for my horse? How would I get up that ridge? I wonder if the landowner lets people ride there. Are horses allowed at that trailhead? Is there room for a horse trailer?* I can occupy myself in a drive across the state, imagining rides on the various hills. Even in the urban areas, I wonder how far the horse people need to drive to find a boarding stable for their horses. Because I know they are there. There are horsemen that work in downtown Seattle. There are horsewomen that work on fishing boats.

There are horse people that work for start-up companies. All of us drive the highways and think of riding.

Dressage riders think of a leg yield when they ask their car to change lanes, maybe briefly reaching for an imaginary whip. Eventers look at the guardrails as an invitation to jump and wonder about the footing on the far side. Cowboys and cowgirls look at the cows and think of how best they would move that herd from one pasture to another. It's all in how you see the world, and the world's full of horse people looking out with a soft horseman's eye.

Money Money Money

When I am planning to haul my horse somewhere I always make sure to fill my truck with gas ahead of time. I usually leave my purse at home and carry my little cloth pouch with my phone, driver's license, a credit card, a compass, and my drugs of choice (some Sudafed for sinus problems and ibuprofen for headaches). That gets me through most minor emergencies.

But sometimes, I don't have time to get gas the night before, or I'm extra tired, and I procrastinate. I'm a skilled procrastinator. On those days, I build in time to get gas before leaving town. A month ago I had one of those days. I planned to pick up my neighbor Carol and her horse, get gas on the way, and head an hour and a half southwest to meet friends and ride at Lakeview Ranch, near Odessa. After stopping at Carol's and getting her horse and gear loaded, she stepped up into the truck cab and handed me 25 bucks to chip in for gas.

"No, it's okay, I'm buying the gas," I said.

She insisted, so I suggested she put it in the glove box for a future emergency.

We drove 15 minutes to the gas station. I pulled my phone out of my little pouch and reached for my credit card. It wasn't there. I forgot to transfer it from purse to pouch.

"Um, Carol, I don't have a credit card."

"Oh no," she said, "I didn't bring my wallet."

I had a quarter tank of gas in the truck. Horse trucks eat gas like a stressed and frazzled middle-aged woman eats chocolate. We were running late. I was calculating the time to head home, grab the card and return versus maybe calling my hubby to bring it to me. Then we remembered the cash. Twenty-five bucks at $3.40 a gallon. We scrounged around for extra cash in the console and glove box: nothing. I put the $25 worth of gas in the truck. It bumped the gauge up to a bit more than half a tank. I asked Carol to calculate whether we could get to Odessa. She figured at 10 miles per gallon, we could make it there, and potentially back, although it was tight. I didn't tell her that on one trip my beast of a truck got eight miles per gallon, but that was on the interstate, with trailer and camper at 70 miles per hour. For this trip we were planning to go rural highways and back roads, so surely we should get 10 or more miles per gallon. I hoped. Plus, we were also meeting friends in two other rigs there and I knew they would have some cash to loan. We checked the time again.

"Let's do it!"

I headed the rig down Highway 2, trying not to be a lead foot as I watched the gas gauge creep down. That's the other thing about horse-hauling rigs, you can practically see the needle move as you drive. It can be unnerving. I tried not to think about what we would do if somehow our friends didn't meet us. But, worst case, we could make it home. Barely. On fumes. I imagined what would happen if we really ran out of gas. Would someone stop for us? I thought yes because we were hauling horses. Horse people would stop.

We continued down the quiet and lightly traveled roads to Odessa. We debated whether we should follow the navigator directions from Carol's phone or follow the written directions our friend had sent. The phone directions might be shorter and save some gas, or they might take us on a road that doesn't exist. We decided to follow the written directions, the known quantity. We drove through Odessa, and didn't see a single gas station, at least not on that end of town. We took the jog in the road to head up to the ranch.

At last, we arrived, with three eighths of a tank left. Again, I figured we could make it home on fumes, although I didn't want to try it. I was sure we could make it to Davenport, two-thirds of the way home, and we knew that town had a gas station. Once the other riders arrived, I explained my predicament. Out of the other three riders they scrounged up a total of 23 dollars. That's it. Five adult women with 23 dollars in cash between them. We were rolling in dough. Horsewomen are rich in experiences, not in cash. Nonetheless, that small influx of cash would make all the difference. Thank you, kind ladies!

We went for our ride, had snacks, and headed home. I watched my gas gauge the whole way to Davenport. We bought 23 dollars' worth of gas at the corner station. I was pleased that we would be able to make it home, and also pleased that our friends had come through with some cash. I decided, though, to add a credit card to my list of things to pack for a horse trip. Now all I have to do is remember to check my list. After I find my list.

I also decided I should carry extra emergency money in my phone case. I had a little debate with myself on how much emergency money it should be. Really, 20 bucks doesn't go far in a truck's gas tank. It should be at least 40. Fifty would be even better, but no horse person ever has a $50 bill laying around. The slot in my phone case is small, so more than two folded bills was getting bulky. I settled on two $20 bills.

I finally remembered to pay back the friend that loaned me the twenty dollars a few weeks later, and as I'm writing this I can't remember if I paid the three dollars back to my other friend. I better check. Recently, a different friend hauled my horse and I out to a ride along Long Lake. I offered to chip in for gas, and guess what? I actually had some cash tucked into my phone case and was able to give her some money right then and there. I think I replaced the money in my phone case when I got home. Hmmm . . . I better go check on that. Hopefully, I won't forget my credit card again, let alone leave filling the gas tank to the last minute. But if it does happen, I'll have my emergency cash stash. Always be prepared!

Photography on Horseback

Picture this: it's early summer, a warm day, and my friend Carol and I are on horseback in the pine forest along the Spokane River. Ahead I see Carol's paint horse framed between pines, purple lupines line the trail, and the river glistens in the sun behind her. I ask her to stop, rein my own horse to a stop, pull my smartphone out of my shoulder pouch, frown at it, try to remember where the camera app is, juggle the phone with one hand, try to keep my horse standing quietly with my other hand, frame the picture, admire the view, take several pictures as I wait for Carol's mare to perk her ears forward for the perfect picture—finally there it is! Just then my food-oriented Fjord Horse decides he has had enough of standing still and steps forward, reaching down for some grass as I try to pull him up while snapping pictures one-handed, and Carol's horse decides she has stood still long enough, too. This is my life as a horseback photographer. My friends take all these stunning well-thought-out pictures, and I accidentally take a blurry picture of a rock. I am famous for failed photographs among my riding friends.

Even off a horse, I've never been a good photographer. If you add my photography skills to the back of a moving horse, I can really wow you. I have taken horseback pictures of the ground, or of one of my horse's ears when I was aiming for the person riding ahead of me. I have taken pictures of the inside of my jacket pocket, and the inside of my camera pouch. I have taken crooked pictures of a tree trunk, when I was aiming at the staged photo of my friend's horse standing nicely in front of a lovely meadow with a mountain background. Now and then I have successfully taken a really nice photo of a horse with beautiful scenery, only to find out later that I cut the rider's head off. I have taken what I thought were ten good pictures of a horse, and ended up with only two, one of which was blurry, and in the other the horse's ears were laid back. I don't think about the photos, I just point, click, and cross my fingers that it will be stupendous.

I always thought taking pictures was easy, even more so now with digital cameras and ever-present smartphones. I figured if I took enough pictures, several of them would turn out well. Not necessarily. I am now on a mission to improve my trail-riding photography skills. Below, are some steps I hope will improve my skills.

1. Teach my horse to stand.

I am a rider, not a trainer. But we all need to work on our training skills to deal with circumstances on the trail. I have learned from trainers and instructors to teach the horse skills ahead of time. I should not go out on a trail ride, and ask my horse to stop and stand, unless I have practiced it at home. I need to have a plan for what to do when he is not obedient, and the plan is not to hurry up and try to take five more pictures as he is moving forward and I am pulling him up to stop again. I need to be willing to give up those pictures and focus on the horse until he learns to stand quietly. I need to practice stopping and standing at home until his response is consistent.

For my current horse, if he's not listening to me, I need to back him up, or put him to work on trot circles until he is ready to stand quietly where I place him. That may not be the answer for your horse but find what his answer is and practice until he responds to your request. Practice at home, then ride with a patient friend and practice it on the trail. If your horse isn't ready to stand still from the saddle, dismount to take your award-winning trail pictures. Your buddies will appreciate their non-blurry pictures.

2. Know my camera.

My camera is usually my smartphone. But I am a stupid user of a smartphone, and sometimes I'm not sure if I have successfully taken one picture, let alone ten. I need to practice at home with my phone's camera, without the horse, so I can quickly set it up and be sure I am successful. I'm going to be practicing many things this riding year.

3. Determine the rules of thumb for setting up a good photo.

I looked around the internet for a simple list of the top five hints for taking better pictures on camera phones. There are many hints, far more than five, and not all are simple. The problem for me is I can only keep three things in my brain at a time, especially when riding and being aware of what my horse is doing. I plan to start with just a couple of those hints and once I get those down maybe I can add on to my list. The following are a few ideas I might be able to keep in my over-filled brain:

- Notice the light. Bright light shows off a face, so the sun should usually be behind the photographer. But the brightest conditions may make your subjects squint so light shade might be better. Explore the best angle for the light conditions.
- Look at the horizon. Is it where I want it in the picture? Is it straight?
- Think about the composition. Is the horse centered in that stunning landscape? Is the rider's head cut off? Should I move back to show more scenery, or forward to show more horse?

4. Notice the horse's expression.

Get those horse ears facing forward. All horses are beautiful when their ears are perked. Once I have the photo staged and the camera ready, I need to pause. "Come on pretty horse, perk those ears!" Maybe if I wave a bandana at the other horse . . . Yes, one more thing to practice at home, so my horse doesn't shy from the scary, attacking bandana as I end up taking a picture of my horse's belly on my way to the ground.

5. Take several pictures.

It's hard to tell on a small digital screen whether a photo is really in focus, or if the rider's head is cut off. Okay, maybe I could figure out the last part if I actually looked, but I don't have time; we have miles to go before I sleep. I don't check closely until I get back home, when it's too late to fix it. It seems like I have a better chance of success with lots of pictures. Well, most people do, anyhow.

My photographs aren't going to get better just by wishing. I'll need to work at it. I suppose it's like so many things in life—we get better with practice (as do our horses). Even if I never get better, and all my horsey-friends continue to tease me about my poor photography skills, I'll still have memories of the best views in the world—the view down the trail from the back of a horse.

Trying to take a bad photo. Photo credit Carol Klar.

Getting Lost

I get lost all the time. I don't really like to call it getting lost, though, it's more being misplaced in space and time. I usually know where I am, it's just not where I meant to be. There's always something new around the corner of that road I've never been on, so it's all a good thing. My penchant for being lost does cause me to be late now and then.

Part of my ability to get lost stems from trying to squeeze too much into my day, and frantically running to the car before double checking the location's address. Even for places I've been to before, if it's not in my neighborhood I like to confirm the street number. Otherwise, I'm not always sure if I take a different crossroad in. Do I turn left, or right on the street to get to that friend of a friend's house?

Another part of my ability to get lost is due to the weird way my brain works. I travel by landmarks, not road names. I don't actually recognize the landmarks until I get to them. In my brain, I am a mouse, and the world is a maze, and I only see the part in front of my nose on that journey to get to the cheese. But I can smell the cheese and recognize each new corner as long as I've traveled that part of the maze a couple times before. Except when the landmarks, or the maze corners, look the same. This happened a few weeks ago, when I was traveling to my writers' group at a house I go to a few times each year. I always get on the freeway and think, *Is it the Salnave exit, or the Tyler exit?* That day I approached the correct exit and tried to recognize a landmark in the pine forest before the exit. As I drove past not recognizing anything distinctive or dramatic, I finally thought, *I think that was it.* But I was past it by then. The next exit was Tyler, a few miles further, so I pulled off there and thought, *Wrong exit. But will it be quicker if I just take this frontage road back? I wonder . . .* Whereupon I called my husband, who has that other kind of brain, the one with a grid-map of the world in it. I asked him if I could get to there from here. Sure, he said, turn right on Ritchey and left on Baker. Or whatever those road names were. I've already forgotten. I did what he said even though it felt wrong and took a jaunt on the dirt roads of rural Spokane County. Who knew there were so many cattle ranches out that way?

I drove a while, took a 90-degree left, and never found Baker. I called my friend to check in on location and admit I was lost. Again. She guided me back to her house. My husband had sent me the wrong way, although he later claimed it was because I had not specifically clarified my starting point. I still blame him. Although I do admit if I had just doubled back on the freeway, I would have been fine.

Yet another part of my ability to get lost is due to my lack of knowledge of the cardinal directions. It wasn't too long after the writers' group highway exit fiasco when my friend Carol and I took our horses up to Mount Spokane to ride. At the time Carol was new to the area, and I had been wanting to ride up there for years. I preferred to do the ride with someone who knew the trails, however it hadn't worked out that summer, and the weather was perfect, and time was a-wasting. Carol may have started to have her doubts when I admitted I hadn't slept the night before and was kind of spacey, and I pulled my truck and trailer the wrong direction on the main road out of our neighborhood. I then did a U-turn, with full truck and trailer through the nearby casino parking lot. But I got us headed the right way and eventually the coffee started kicking in and I finally found Mt. Spokane.

We headed to the cross-country ski area because I knew the trails were moderately hilly and wide and there was a huge parking lot to unload our horses. Plus, I had skied there before and knew the trails were well-marked and color-coded and that they looped out and around and came back to major junction points with big map displays. In addition, I had planned ahead and had brought a map of the area. I did not, however, have a compass that day. No matter, I can read a map, and Carol has a spatial and mathematical brain, and she can read a map and it was all good. What could go wrong?

We saddled up and headed out on a perfect fall day. At the first major junction in the trail, I mentally noted a gravel road that headed back to the parking lot and remembered skiing that way long ago. It was a direct route back. We rode out further along the ski trails. These were trails as wide as roads so we could ride side by side. We had great views, beautiful weather, and we followed the map boards to a closed-up warming hut, and then continued out around Baldy Knob.

After a couple hours we thought we should head back. We were just delighted with our ride, our horses were great, and we came to a junction with a gate and a gravel road. I was sure that was the way back to the parking lot, so we took that gravel road. We trotted, we cantered, we rode, then rode some more and came to another junction in the road with a big display map with a "you are here" dot. And we were way off from where I thought we should be. We looked at the map. Looked at the road. Looked at my paper map. Looked at the peak of Mount Spokane in the distance. Figured out which way was west from the shadows in the late afternoon. Looked at the stream on the map that was between us and where we should be, and the steep contour lines. A stream would mean thick brush and there was no direct trail through it marked on either of the maps. Our tired horses were not up to a bush-whacking cross-country climb. We were probably only a quarter mile north of our starting point, but we needed to backtrack three miles or more to get there. I checked the time, and worried briefly about how much food I had in my saddle bags and hoped that my flashlight batteries were still good in case the night caught us on the trail.

We headed back. We tested one trail on the way that looked like it should go the right direction. It looped back to the road we were on. We continued riding all the way back to the junction with the gate, crossed back around the gate, rode back down a trail, and eventually came to one of the major trail junctions with another display map. What was weird, was the map seemed to me to head us the wrong way. Carol's spatial math brain read it, got it, and she turned left, heading back. My landmark-remembering, intuitive brain really wanted to go right. I stared at that map, and at the trail, and finally agreed to follow Carol. In another half-hour we were back at the truck. We made it with daylight to spare! It was all good. But a few days later my husband brought home a compass for me to hang on my saddle.

Plan B (B Is for Breakfast!)

I learned about the philosophy of Plan B in college when I was taking scuba lessons. Our teacher said you must always have a Plan B for your dive, because even with the best planning, reading of tide charts, and reviewing of weather reports, going underwater in bad conditions is not worth your life. If you miscalculated the tides and your dive site currents look like they could pull you to Japan, DON'T DIVE. Whenever you arrive at a dive site, you throw a stick in the water, and see what it does. If it hangs in a slack tide, your planning and timing is perfect. If alternatively, it heads down the coast with the speed of a surf boarder on a big wave, then you move on to Plan B. Plan B might be a tour of a nearby park, going out to breakfast, or walking the docks to admire the sailboats in the harbor.

I have ingrained the idea of Plan B into my life. I have applied this theory to family camping trips. If you're camping and the rain pours down and your tent floods and the sleeping bags are soaked, by all means, pack up your tent and head out to the nearest small town for Plan B. In that instance, Plan B is for breakfast in a busy and yummy small-town restaurant.

My neighbor Carol and I do a lot of horseback rides together and sometimes they don't work out quite how we planned. There's always a Plan B for trail riding, too. If we go riding at the state park and my aged horse is acting like an untrained toddler, or as Carol puts it, Oly's fire-breathing-dragon mode, Plan B might be working from the ground, or riding in the arena instead of continuing the trail ride. Or, if you show up at a trailhead, and your horse is lame, or threw a shoe, Plan B might be to have a piece of pie, or a glass of beer in the nearest restaurant. Horses can stand in the trailer for an hour, and if they can't, it's time they learned.

One of my teachers says to always have a lawn chair and a book with you. If your horse is acting up even before saddling and it seems risky to get on, don't. This is the equivalent of throwing the stick in the ocean to check the current. If your horse's emotional current is looking too strong, then Plan B is for book. Tie the horse solid and read your book while your friends go out for a ride. Eventually your horse will stand, and you'll catch up on your reading.

Plan B shouldn't be a disappointment or a ruined day because something went wrong. Plan B is just a different kind of fun activity or adventure. Without Plan B, I wouldn't have made it to a lot of really good breakfast restaurants all over the state. Now that I think about it, my favorite Plan B probably is breakfast, even in the middle of the day. Sometimes the unplanned alternatives are just as fun as the original event. Plus, hashbrowns!

Comedy of Errors

Fjord Horses come in five colors, with the most common one being "brown dun." Both Oly and Vali are brown duns. I'm not sure how people with a whole herd of brown dun Fjord Horses tell them apart. I can tell Vali and Oly apart, most of the time, if I'm paying attention. If they are out in the pasture at a distance, they look the same.

Up close I can tell them apart because Oly has a wider jaw and shorter face, a bigger eye, and a poofy forelock. He is cute. Vali has a longer face, and a longer poofy forelock. He is handsome. Oly's back is as wide as an easy chair, and Vali's back is more triangular and not at all comfortable for bareback riding. Oly's fur is a little darker, and thick and coarse like wool. Vali's is finer and softer, and not as long in the winter. Oly's mane is very wide across the top of the neck, Vali's mane is narrower. Oly is thicker and a little shorter in build. But if I'm not looking closely and going through my checklist of differences, I sometimes grab the wrong horse. I usually notice right away, laugh at myself, and go back for the correct horse.

One spring day I had a riding lesson scheduled after work. I was running a little late and was in a hurry. I checked the trailer to make sure I had all the necessary gear, then ran to Vali's paddock, haltered him, and loaded him in the trailer. I got stopped at a train crossing, so was even later to arrive at the barn for my lesson.

I parked my rig and didn't see my instructor Regina in the outdoor arena. I figured she was giving a lesson indoors and I would find her once I was tacked up. I opened the back door of the trailer, stepped in and opened the divider to the front stall. I saw my horse staring back at me curiously, fuzzy ears perked, with big eyes. I looked at his flat broad back. Oly looked back at me, smiling in a horse sort of way. Oly had been in Vali's paddock, and I grabbed the wrong horse.

I paused to think. I can use the same bridle on both horses, but not the same saddle. Plus, Oly was semi-retired at the time, and somewhat lame. I could do a bareback walking lesson, however Oly didn't need the work like Vali did. I closed up the trailer, texted Regina explaining my mistake, then texted my husband to have Vali haltered and ready. I headed back home, a 15-minute haul.

Back at home, my husband and I efficiently swapped out the horses and I headed back to the stable. I hadn't heard from Regina yet. When I arrived back at the barn, I still didn't see Regina. I texted Regina again, announcing my arrival with the correct horse. I wasn't concerned—there's always a Plan B—and this time it was to ride my young goofy horse in a big arena. Soon I got a text from Regina that she was on her way. Eventually she arrived, laughing. She couldn't believe I brought the wrong horse, and somehow, she had missed the lesson on her calendar. She had left the barn right before I arrived late with the first horse and missed my first text. By this point Vali was well warmed-up since we had already walked, trotted, and cantered. We ended up with a great lesson after the comedy of errors.

I learned from that day of the wrong horse. I started trimming each horse's mane differently, to add one more very obvious difference between them. Now I trim the white part of Oly's bicolor mane short, and the black part remains tall, so it looks like he has a black mohawk. I trim Vali's mane so it is white on the outside, to contrast with Oly's. But I still must pay attention, especially when they walk into the wrong paddock after I turn them out, which happens often. I'm starting to think the horses pick the wrong paddock on purpose, their own kind of April fool's trick.

I haltered the wrong horse again recently but noticed it just before loading him into the trailer. I was quite sure both horses were laughing at me.

Then there was the day I was hauling to my friend's house to trail ride and in preparation I backed the trailer into the driveway to get it headed the right direction. I started pulling out toward my destination when I realized I hadn't actually loaded the horse yet. Not the wrong horse, not the right horse, no horse whatsoever. That would have been really embarrassing. Luckily no one knows about that.

Vali and Oly with Michelle and Carol Klar aboard.
Photo credit Carol Klar.

Dear Santa

Late last winter I left the laptop in the barn while I was riding Vali. This is what I found typed on the computer when I returned. I'm not exactly sure how Oly typed it, but horses' noses are extremely agile.

Dear Santa,

We share some heritage, you and me. Kris Kringle is Scandinavian, right? And the Christmas tree came from Scandinavia too, right? I am a Norwegian Fjord Horse, so we're practically cousins. Plus, your reindeer come from Scandinavia. I like the deer here in Washington State. Our deer don't fly, at least not higher than a fence. Sometimes I try to walk up to one to say, "Hi," but they don't want me to get too close. I blame my rider. You know that saying, it's always the rider's fault? It's true. Always.

I'm writing to tell you my Christmas list. I would like horse treats. And hay. And carrots. Don't give me any apples though, because I know they're just a way for my owner to sneak medicine in. No bran for the same reason. But anything else edible sounds great to me. Bring lots of it! I'm so tired of the diet my owner keeps me on. It has made me so anxious I have started eating the fence boards. Heck, I would nibble on a Christmas tree if you brought me one. Maybe we could decorate it with horse cookies?

My pasture mate, Vali, also wants food. He eats everything. Sometimes he kicks at me, so bring some red ribbons to put in his tail. It will remind me not to get too close. We could both use some new horse boots that fit, the rubbery kind. That way we can kick each other and I won't get hurt. It keeps the rocks from bothering our feet, too, when we get to go out on the road. I love to go out for rides! My owner has been neglecting me since Vali showed up. Sometimes I have such an urge to kick Vali back.

My rider needs some winter riding pants and gloves, so she doesn't hide in the house all winter. She is not blessed with thick fur like us

Fjord Horses. Poor thing. We like it when she comes out to visit. Oh, and get her one of those books about feeding horses the natural way, the one that says we should have free choice hay available all the time. Plus, she needs a natural horsemanship book that shows her how to be the dominant boss mare. Not to use on me, I'm perfect. Vali can be a spoiled brat though; he needs discipline.

For the owner's husband, maybe you could bring some new lead ropes. We like to go for walks with him; he lets us graze. If you bring horse treats, be sure to tell him where they are. He shares better than our owner.

For the teenage boy, bring some brushes. If he gets busy and stressed at school, he can come outside and brush us. It would make us—I mean him—feel happy.

For the dog, well, that dog is kinda bothersome. She spends all her time trying to get the chickens, and mostly ignores us horses. Get her a lead rope too, and maybe the humans will take her for more walks. She is good at cleaning up our hoof trimmings though. Maybe bring her some chew toys to occupy her between trimmings.

And then there's the barn kitty. We don't see him much; he seems to be trying to become a house kitty. I don't know why, since he has thick fur like us, and should be plenty warm. Maybe a catnip mouse would remind him that his job is to keep the mice from eating our food.

Really, Santa, I just wanted to give you some ideas of what to bring on Christmas. We don't have a chimney in the barn to slide down, but we'll be watching for you. We like standing out in the cold under the stars. If you have an extra minute, I'd love to sniff noses with the reindeer.

Merry Christmas and Happy New Year!

Sincerely,
Oly the Elder

P.S. Don't forget the horse treats.

Everything I Need to Know I Learned from My Horse

A good friend once said, "Animals are put on this earth to teach you something." I think back on my time with horses and I believe she was right. Here are some of the things I have learned from my horses, and how those lessons relate to me.

Grazing is good.

Horses' digestive systems are such that they do best if they are eating roughage frequently. If they get high calorie meals less frequently, sometimes they have issues such as ulcers. Or they develop bad habits, like chewing on wood. Also, to keep that digestive system working, they need access to water, all the time.

I do better when I graze all day too, and even better if I feed myself a lot of roughage. If I don't eat healthy snacks frequently during the day, I crash. So, modeling my eating after a horse is a good thing.

Friends keep you calm.

This is especially true of my current younger horse. He is at his best if he has a horse friend nearby. He gets nervous without one. He should become more confident with more work. In the meantime, friends matter.

It's the same for me—friends matter. Although I like my alone time, I also need friend time. Imagine life without friends. It would definitely make me anxious just like it does most horses.

Hills are for climbing. Fast.

Most horses, faced with a steep hill, prefer to run up it. I'm not sure why, but it's fun when you're on their back.

When I'm faced with a big obstacle at work, or in my personal life, I'll often look for an easy way around, however, in the end, I must face that hill and climb. Most obstacles require you to march right over them.

Sunbathing feels good.

Even in the winter, after breakfast, my horses will go out and bask in the sun, soaking up that radiant heat.

Even in the winter, nothing feels better for me than some sunny warmth, whether outside or through a window. It gives me hope that spring will come, and I can get out with the horses.

Snow angels, mud angels, and dust angels.

Rolling around feels great. Horses are forever rolling in the dirt, snow, or mud. They are scratching their itches. There's an old saying that every time a horse rolls all the way over, you count $100 in value. I had a horse once, Joaquin, that rolled over 14 times in a row; $1,400 was an expensive horse at the time. For today's horse prices, I think it should be $1,000 per roll.

From the horses I've learned, if you have an itch, scratch it. Do what feels good.

It feels good to have clean feet.

Horses have these deep divots in their hooves, on either side of their frog (the fleshy V-shaped part of the underside of the hoof). They need cleaning with a hoof-pick. I'm not really sure that it feels good to them, but it ensures that there are no nails or rocks in their feet that could induce lameness.

For me, the equivalent is hosing the grit and dirt off my feet and sandals after walking in the garden soil in the summer. Nothing feels better. Around the horses though? I wear boots.

Flies are a bother.

Flies flitter around. They suck moisture out of a horses' eyes. They grow in manure. Some chew up the inside of horses' ears. There are no redeeming qualities.

As for human's views on flies? Ditto.

Meet me where I am.

You can't hurry training. Trust takes time. Some horses are easy to train and some horses are hard to train. But, if you force them too fast, you leave holes that will show up later. You need to train in slow steps, at the horse's speed.

For me, this is the equivalent of living in the moment. If you and your horse aren't ready for a large group trail ride, don't do it. Find another quieter activity for now, even if it's a walk down the road with your equine buddy.

Life is short.

If you're a horse, it's good to be young, and it's good to be old, and it's especially good to eat grass. Life is short, eat grass now.

For me, life is short, ride now. And eat brownies.

It's the Journey

The journey of a thousand miles begins with one step.
—*Lao Tzu*

Horsemanship is a journey of learning and training. Some days I really notice how far Vali and I have come. Some days I wonder if we'll ever get to where I want us to be. Some days on a quiet trail, I simply appreciate where we are and enjoy the moment. Horse Zen.

Vali started as a green broke horse, who wasn't really broke at all, and was spoiled and opinionated. We got help, and moved on to the mostly predictable, although sometimes erratically worried, stage of riding. Then, by the third year of our journey, we reached the pretty-darn-good trail horse stage of riding. Except when there are large groups or strange noises, or if another horse suddenly runs up to us, or suddenly runs away from us. Perhaps we just aren't meant for large groups. Other times, Vali is the calm one, the old hand, the steadying influence. He will go over any trail obstacle I point him at, like a mountain goat. Maybe we aren't meant for perfection.

We have come far. Each year I assess where we want to go and what we want to do. We can always continue working on independence and ability to leave and rejoin a group. We can always work on more speed and energy. I can always work on softness and sitting straight in the saddle.

One spring a friend's horse was caught in a bog. It was frightening watching the horse fight to get out of the belly-deep mud. He made it out, but was exhausted. I had to ride away from the small group of horses, to go get my trailer and move it closer. That was a tense ride on a coiled spring, our first ride away from a group. It took all of my riding skill to keep Vali from leaping and bolting back to his buddies. But we did it. There was a time when I couldn't even have done that, when the leap would have happened, and I would've been tossed. The tense ride was progress, a step on the journey to independence and confidence on both our parts. I see a much longer path ahead, to ride to my goal of a finished and independent trail horse.

Perfection is probably overrated. Like bomb-proof, it's a myth. I think

I will just aim for "solid" trail horse. Besides, if my horse was perfect, what would I laugh at? There's always something to work on, something to learn, another step in our journey of many miles. For now, I ride one step at a time, feeling the back and forth of the horse's stride, the side-swaying of his barrel. Whether it's in the arena, on a wilderness trail, down the road, or grabbing a few minutes bareback in the round pen, my riding time keeps me sane. I see more trails, more trials, and more laughter ahead.

A Horse's Blessing

May you have clear paths, soft footing, and room to canter.
May all downed logs in your path be free of branches to make a joyful jump.
May your springs be wet enough to grow hay and summers dry enough for good harvests.
May your pasture have shade in summer and a warm barn in winter.
May your pasture be filled with green grass and a running stream for fresh water.

So many trails, so little time. Michelle and Vali.
Photo credit Carol Klar.

Acknowledgments

I am grateful to the editors of publications where a few of my manuscripts were previously published, sometimes in different versions:

centaurlit.com: Horse Breeding, Vegas Style

Horse and Rider Magazine: Kodo's Secret Life

PKA Advocate: Saddle Shopping

Several other pieces have been published as blog posts or in the newsletter for the local Ponderosa chapter of the Back Country Horseman of Washington.

About the Author

Photo credit Cindy Miller.

Michelle Eames writes poetry, humor, and essays about a broad range of topics, including biology, horsemanship, and wildfires. She has published in *Flyway*, *Pontoon*, *Earthspeak*, *PKA Advocate*, *Horse and Rider Magazine*, *Backyard Poultry*, and various journals, newsletters, and online locations. Michelle lives on a hobby farm near Spokane, Washington, with two horses, two barn cats that strive to be house cats, a few chickens, and a husband. When she isn't writing, riding, or shoveling manure, Michelle spends her time gardening, up-cycling wool sweaters, and repairing vintage sewing machines to keep them out of landfills.

Website and Blog:
MichelleEames.com

www.ingramcontent.com/pod-product-compliance
Lightning Source LLC
Chambersburg PA
CBHW060532130626
46553CB00002B/719